Surgeon with the Kaiser's Army

Surgeon with the Kaiser's Army

Stephan Kurt Westmann

Edited by
Michael Stephen Westman

Pen & Sword
MILITARY

First published in Great Britain by
PEN AND SWORD MILITARY
an imprint of
Pen and Sword Books Ltd
47 Church Street
Barnsley
South Yorkshire S70 2AS

Copyright © Michael Stephen Westman 2014

ISBN 978 1 47382 170 5

Printed and bound in England by
CPI Group (UK) Ltd, Croydon, CR0 4YY

Typeset in Times by CHIC GRAPHICS

Pen & Sword Books Ltd incorporates the imprints of
Pen & Sword Books Ltd incorporates the imprints of Pen & Sword
Archaeology, Atlas, Aviation, Battleground, Discovery,
Family History, History, Maritime, Military, Naval, Politics,
Railways, Select, Social History, Transport, True Crime, and
Claymore Press, Frontline Books, Leo Cooper, Praetorian Press,
Remember When, Seaforth Publishing and Wharncliffe.

For a complete list of Pen and Sword titles please contact
Pen and Sword Books Limited
47 Church Street, Barnsley, South Yorkshire, S70 2AS, England
E-mail: enquiries@pen-and-sword.co.uk
Website: www.pen-and-sword.co.uk

Contents

Introduction

I can just remember my grandfather Stephan Westmann when I was a little boy. He was kindly and greeted me warmly in his heavily German-accented English. We played chess together and his Hertfordshire home was full of interesting artefacts from his life as a surgeon in Germany and Britain.

After he died in 1964, the interviews he gave to camera as part of the BBC *Great War* series were broadcast into Britain's homes. It was the days of black and white television and the series had been made to commemorate fifty years since the start of the 'war to end all wars'.

As an adult, it began to dawn on me that this man had led a double life. Born into a well-to-do Berlin family in 1893, he had volunteered for the Kaiser's army as a young medical student while at Freiburg University. That he survived over four years in the front line has always amazed me. One of life's high achievers, he won both Iron Crosses and a hatful of other medals for the Fatherland. He proved his mettle on the front line, killing enemy soldiers in gruesome hand-to-hand combat and then as a medical officer saving the lives of many others – British as well as German. After the war, being both an outspoken anti-Nazi and Jewish, he was among a number of prominent Berliners whom the Nazis wished to silence as soon as they seized power in 1933 and he fled to Britain prior to the start of the Second World War.

The names of the battlefields where he served will be familiar to all school-age historians and those with an interest in the First World War. What is different about this book is that it was written from a German perspective. As a first-language English speaker myself, I have rewritten my grandfather's book from start to finish, updating the language and the word order in particular. It seems that he wrote the original in German and then had it translated; it is this translation from which I have worked. However, I have been careful to leave in the author's first-hand experiences and the views and attitudes of others – warts and all. His writing (wonderfully politically incorrect by today's standards) covers the social, political, intellectual, religious, medical and economic aspects of wartime life under the Kaiser in vivid detail. His views remain as he wrote them in the early 1960s.

It is hoped that this book will give the reader a further insight into the prevailing politics and zeitgeist and life from the 'enemy' side of the First World War. It has been rewritten to commemorate one hundred years since that awful war started.

Michael Stephen Westman
Skye
October 2013

Part I
(1914)

If, therefore, war should ever come between these two countries, which Heaven forbid it will not, I think, be due to irresistible natural laws, it will be due to the want of human wisdom.

Andrew Bonar Law, speech to the House of Commons, November 1911

The events of 1914

28 June	Assassination of the Archduke Franz Ferdinand and his Archduchess in Sarajevo.
30 July	Russia mobilizes.
1 August	Germany declares war on Russia; France and Germany mobilize.
2 August	Germany demands that Belgium give free passage for her troops.
3 August	Germany declares war on France.
4 August	Britain issues ultimatum to Germany over Belgium. War declared at midnight.
11 August	General Joffre invades Alsace with six divisions. Mulhouse taken but then recovered by the Germans.
14 August	French cross Alsatian frontier aiming to attack the Germans from the south. Six days later, the French

armies are driven back towards the frontier by Crown Prince Rupprecht of Bavaria's troops.

| September | The 'Race to the Sea': Allied troops race north and German troops wheel via Belgium, striving to outflank each other. |

10 October — Fall of Antwerp, releasing more German divisions (many volunteers are under the statutory military age) to concentrate their forces near Lille. Rupprecht's troops are brought up from Lorraine.

12 October — British advance between La Bassée and Armentières is beaten back by Rupprecht's infantry. However, great losses inflicted on the Germans.

20 October — The Battle of Yser: the Germans attack across a line from the coastal town of Nieuport to the La Bassée canal.

30 October — The First Battle of Ypres – the 'Massacre of the Innocents'. Great losses sustained by both sides.

11 November — German offensive at Menin Road.

December — Joffre attacks in Artois and Champagne without success.Trench warfare starts.

Chapter 1

'If War Should Ever Come'

The bells of Berlin had rung in the New Year of 1914. Together with some friends, the Westmann family celebrated this event at home on the Kufürstendamm and toasted in the New Year with the traditional '*Prosit Neujahr*'. Everyone was happy and the atmosphere was carefree. We set off some fireworks, told the customary New Year jokes and let loose little tin mice which glided across the floor and under the long skirts of the shrieking *Fräuleins*.

According to another old German tradition, shortly after midnight each of us melted a small piece of lead in an old spoon over a flame. The liquid lead was then quickly poured into a basin of cold water where it immediately formed all kinds of figures resembling ships, people, wild beasts and fantastic mythical creations. Out of these weird shapes we tried to foretell the future and my grandmother Dora was considered an expert in this mystical art. She frowned and predicted tempests and a series of grave events. We did not believe her. On the contrary, we were convinced that the New Year was bound to be happy and prosperous.

Germany under Kaiser Wilhelm II was a hive of activity. The economic boom which had developed after the Franco-Prussian war of 1870□1 had continued and the upward trend in commerce and industry were reflected in a prosperity which pervaded all classes. The enterprising spirit of the middle and upper classes brought them wealth and comfort and the workers seemed content, protected against exploitation by powerful trades unions, a raft of social reforms and legislation passed by the *Reichstag* [Parliament].

Everyone was well fed and well clad. Slums hardly existed, though working class accommodation was generally small. Most people lived in flats, which were generally kept spotlessly clean and well-furnished. Later, as a young doctor, I had ample opportunity to visit these homes and often had to stay in them overnight on domiciliary visits to women giving birth.

Unemployment and illiteracy were virtually non-existent. Certainly, there were political parties in the *Reichstag* with differing aims, aspirations and divergent views but the Kaiser's social and political activity had removed any real threat of class war. The administration appeared to be corruption-free. In 1883 Chancellor Bismarck had created the National Health Insurance programme and this was almost thirty years before Lloyd George visited Germany to study and to use it as a blueprint for the British Health Insurance Scheme.

In all, the Germans on New Year's Day in 1914 comprised an affluent society and had good reason to be satisfied with their lot. The arts and sciences flourished and Germany was a world leader in my chosen profession of medicine. The ordinary German man went quietly about his business. After a hard day's work he and his wife went to his local pub to meet with friends and to drink traditional *Berliner Weiße* or white beer. The slightly sour taste of this naturally cloudy, low-alcohol wheat beer was offset by a dash of raspberry syrup. Served in large flat-bottomed glasses, this refreshing and delicious drink was the social lubricant of the day!

On Sundays in the summertime my father would take us to a coffee garden at one of the many lovely lakes near to Berlin. Mother would bring a large bag full of homemade cakes and pre-ground coffee. At the counter of the coffee house boiling water would be provided and a charge made depending on the number of cups and saucers allocated. The net result was . . . *gemütlichkeit*, for which probably the closest English translation would be a feeling of wellbeing, similar to that experienced in a British pub or French *bistro* or *estaminet*.

What about religion? Well, put simply, we were not a religious family. Certainly we were Jewish by descent though we did not speak Yiddish, let alone Hebrew. In 1914, long before the rise of the Nazis and the name Hitler became known and reviled, people in Berlin worshipped their own God in their own particular way. Churches and synagogues coexisted side by side and anti-semitism was not an issue.

Germany had been at peace for forty-four years since the 1870 war against the French. Following their victory, the Germans demanded from the French restitutions identical to those Napoleon had imposed on

Germany in 1806. In fact, my great-great-grandfather had been forced to give up heirlooms including his gold watch to help pay for this. In 1871 France had to cede her provinces of Alsace-Lorraine, though it must be said that Alsace was typically German. Maps of the area showing historical developments confirm this point. As a young student in Freiburg I often went hiking in the Vosges mountains. I slept in inns and farmhouses where nobody spoke a word of French. Instead they spoke a German dialect similar to the Swiss-German one can hear in Basle. Indeed, the town of Mülhausen belonged to Switzerland for centuries.

Ethnologically, the people of Alsace originate from a German tribe, the Allemans. To this day, the French word for Germans is *(les) Allemands* and for Germany, *Allemagne*. However, after the humiliating defeat of the boastful Napoleon III in 1871, the French became so consumed with hatred for the Germans and the idea of *revanche* [revenge] – 'Never speak of it, always think of it' □ that in Paris on the Place de la Concorde they draped a veil of black material around a female statue representing Strasbourg! At that time, Strasbourg was a typically German town, which personally I knew very well indeed.

Britain had fought a costly war against the Boers only sixteen or so years earlier. The Russians had attacked the Japanese and sustained a bloody defeat. France herself had waged one colonial campaign after another in Cochin China [S.E. Asia] or North Africa. True, there were comparatively few French soldiers involved, as the armies consisted mostly of foreign legionaries, amongst them many German, British, Spanish and God-knows-which nationalities!

Germany had been at peace, and so we slipped merrily into the New Year of 1914. On the morning of 1 January my father went with us on that public holiday to the Kaiser's palace and to the Armoury in Unter den Linden. Here we saw the Kaiser resplendent in his uniform, complete with plumed helmet. He was accompanied by his six sons and son-in-law, Ernest of Brunswick, the Duke of Cumberland. They were all at the War Museum at the Armoury to receive the New Year congratulations of each army unit.

The Kaiser's motto was the old Latin proverb, *Quis desiderat pacem, praeparet bellum:* 'He who desires peace prepares for war.' The Kaiser was actually called the 'Prince of Peace'. One must bear in mind that his *Reich* had two very strong neighbours, i.e. Russia and revenge-seeking France, whose combined armies numbered three million soldiers, at least double that of Germany.

Germany had developed a highly efficient and rapidly expanding industry for which she needed raw materials and export markets. Furthermore, Germany's population had also grown enormously, reaching sixty-five million. She wanted to expand by means of colonialism but was late on the scene to achieve this aim. By contrast, Britain's population was only thirty-eight million but she had a vast colonial empire; Italy had secured Tripolitania, and France, Belgium and Portugal (all of whose populations were declining) tried to enlarge their possessions in Algeria, the Congo and East and West Africa.

Friction developed, leading to the Entente Cordiale between France, Russia and Britain, with Italy and to some extent Belgium as benevolent and not-quite-disinterested bystanders. All of them were jealous of their respective spheres of interest and tried to bar the way to any newcomer wishing to have a slice of the riches of the colonial world. All they conceded to Germany was a few stretches of land in Africa. Most of this was desert, scrub or bushland. This, I think, was the view of the ordinary peace-loving German. It is not for me to decide whether it was right or wrong as I am not an historian. However, at that time I was a student interested in politics and foreign affairs in particular.

Kaiser Wilhelm predicted that the British would use their superior sea power to impose and enforce a blockade on Germany. The French and Russian navies were also looking threatening. On a visit to Swinemünde on the Baltic Sea, I saw for myself a number of large, menacing-looking Russian warships. With this in mind, the Kaiser's efforts to build a navy to be at least a match for the British battle fleet seemed justifiable to the man in the street in Berlin.

Berliners enjoyed watching the big parades on the Tempelhof Field (later to become Berlin Airport). It was a popular sight to see the Kaiser on horseback under a solitary poplar tree, reviewing his troops. Afterwards, the soldiers marched through the streets and down Unter den Linden to the Kaiser's palace. He, like a demigod in the uniform of the *Garde du Corps*, wearing a silver helmet crowned with the Prussian eagle, rode in front of the standard-bearers of the Berlin garrison. Behind him, the massed brass bands of the regiment of the *Garde* were led by a giant African prince carrying the so-called *Schellenbaum*, an emblem similar to that of the Roman legions and adorned with little bells and horsehair plumes. Then followed the battalions of the footguards, some with high silver helmets dating back to the time of Frederick I of Prussia at the end of the seventeenth century.

Bringing up the rear were the cavalry in their splendour. The Cuirassiers wore white uniforms and helmets which rather resembled those of the British Household Cavalry. Behind them rode the Uhlans with their lances and small black and white flags and then the Hussars in red or green dolmans. Near to the pavement rode a horseman in the black uniform of the 'Death's Head Hussars', not shy about waving to any pretty girls in the crowd! This was the Crown Prince, 'Little Willie' as he was often called.

The people lined the streets and cried 'Hurrah'. The Kaiser saluted them with his field marshal's baton whilst he held the reins of his horse with his left hand, hiding his short and withered left arm. In his entourage were many foreign high-ranking officers: Russians, French, British, Italians and even Japanese, in the full splendour of their national uniforms.

I often discussed with my father (a left-wing liberal) the reason why Wilhelm staged such extravagant military spectacles. Surely he was not interested in merely playing 'toy' soldiers; this would have been an extremely expensive business and the *Reichstag* certainly would have vetoed such a waste of money. My father, who was partly of farming stock, explained the position as he saw it: Germany was like a man who owned rich grazing land with hardly any protection from his aggressive neighbours, whom he knew to be jealous and hostile. They were itching for the right moment to jump over his low fences, burn his house and steal his cattle. What could he do to safeguard his property? Most likely he would keep fierce dogs to bite and drive off any trespassers or intruders. He would also fix a large 'Beware of the Dogs' sign on his gate and would even let his acquisitive neighbours see his fierce German sheepdogs for themselves.

Wilhelm was no fool and neither was he suffering from paranoia. He knew exactly what was brewing in the minds of the vengeful French. They had already made several successful insurgencies in the past but had got a good hiding in 1870.

Russia had concentrated huge armies on Germany's eastern borders. She was ruled by a despotic autocrat or Tsar (from the Latin *Caesar,* as is the word Kaiser), entirely dominated by a bellicose, militaristic clique including the mad monk Rasputin. Obviously it was difficult to defend the wide, open plains of eastern Germany against the Russian 'steamroller', and the Cossacks had watered their horses in the Spree, Berlin's river, not so very long ago. Small wonder that the farmers and landowners of these parts of Germany, the Junkers as they were called, pressed for more troops and stronger fortifications for their protection.

Several of my uncles and cousins who lived there and visited us complained that for scores of miles there was not a single army unit and that the Russians would have an almost unopposed walk into the heart of Germany. When war really did break out, they had to flee for their lives, leaving their homesteads to marauding Russian hordes, who promptly plundered them and burnt them down. As it turned out, it was only incredibly bad Russian generalship which saved Berlin, my home town, not two hundred miles from the Russo-Polish frontier.

Britain, on the other hand, was safe and had nothing to fear. Surrounded by the sea, her splendid navy was ready to repel any potential aggressor. Her army comprised some 130,000 men – all professional soldiers, though the bulk of these were stationed overseas, mostly in India. Her traditional policy was to watch with Argus eyes over the so-called balance of power in Europe. According to British perceptions, nobody should be allowed to have clear-cut hegemony over other nations and thus become a challenge to her. Britannia ruled the waves and everything connected, such as her colonies and foreign markets. The leading exponent of this strategy was Britain's King Edward VII, who saw a potential competitor in his nephew, i.e. Kaiser Wilhelm II of Germany.

Here it might be appropriate to take a closer look at the British King and the German Kaiser as *we* saw them from my family's perspective. My father had close business connections with Britain. He had lived there and visited about twice yearly. He told us of the many stories which had circulated of the scandals and love affairs of the then Prince of Wales. The already ageing Prince was forbidden by his mother Queen Victoria from taking part in top-level politics because she did not trust his sense of responsibility or discretion. So his main occupation was that of playboy and this at a time when his elegant, good-looking and intelligent nephew Wilhelm had, at the age of twenty-nine, ascended the throne of one of the mightiest powers in the world.

Wilhelm had been reigning for almost thirteen years when Edward took the British throne. Under Wilhelm's rule, Germany had made unprecedented progress in trade, industry, science and the arts. Her population had grown to over sixty million in comparison to Britain's thirty-eight and France's thirty-six million. No wonder the British King saw his nephew as a rival whom he envied and reviled – consciously or not.

Like his uncle Edward, Wilhelm was half German and half British. Edward's father was Prince Albert of Saxe-Coburg-Gotha. Wilhelm's mother was the eldest daughter of the British Queen, Victoria, and, indeed, 'William' was the favourite grandson of the Grand Old Lady. Needlesss to say, Wilhelm spoke perfect English and had both German and British tutors, who initiated him into the intricacies and advantages of the British parliamentary system and the constitutional law of Germany. Bonn was his university. He hated his British mother, who mistreated him psychologically. Incompetent obstetricians had injured his left arm at birth and ignorant surgeons were unable to correct this. His mother often called him a cripple in the presence of other people. Therefore, quite understandably, he developed an inferiority complex for which later he overcompensated by a kind of hauteur which many misinterpreted as arrogance.

On the other hand, he adored his extremely handsome father, Crown Prince Frederick, whose political leanings were towards left-wing liberalism. However, in 1887 the Crown Prince lost his voice and the Regius Professor of Surgery at the University of Berlin, von Bergmann, diagnosed a malignant tumour and wanted to operate at once. The Crown Princess, however, insisted on consulting the British throat surgeon Sir Morell Mackenzie, who declared the growth to be benign and advised against an operation. Barely ten months later, Frederick III, as he had by then become, was dead after a reign of only ninety-nine days. His father Wilhelm I had lived to the ripe old age of ninety-one, and now the twenty-nine-year-old Wilhelm II had to ascend the throne of Germany.

His social policy brought him into conflict with the ultra-conservative

Chancellor Bismarck, and he decided to drop the old pilot from the bridge and take the wheel of the ship of state into his own hands. One must not forget how different the German monarchy was to the British. Whereas in Britain the monarchy has to be impartial and above party politics, in Germany the crowned head really ruled.

Germany was a federal state, comprising twenty-five members under the supreme control of a Federal Council or *Reichsrat*, with Prussia in a majority. Her king also had the title of German Kaiser though not of Kaiser of Germany. He had the power to declare war, but aggressive wars required the consent of the Federal Council. He could sign peace treaties and was the supreme commander of the armed forces. He thus represented the German *Reich* in her relations with other countries, and as such he tried to approach Britain and conclude a treaty of friendship with her and Russia.

However, here his antagonist Edward VII crossed his path and prevented Wilhelm's idea of a great Continental Federation to include Russia and bring about an alleviation of Franco-German tensions which threatened war. Britain's King travelled hither and yon attending conferences in Biarritz, Homburg, Paris and elsewhere, and all of this in addition to his other 'activities'. Finally, he succeeded in concluding alliances with France in 1904 and Russia in 1907.

The British public strongly disapproved of this strategy, regarding France as corrupt and as Britain's traditional foe. The Liberal Government under Sir Henry Campbell-Bannerman had been in office since December 1905. It did not have the nerve to inform the country, Parliament or even some Cabinet ministers that talks had already started between the French and the British general staffs. The entente with Russia was equally unpopular, largely on account of the Tsarist tyranny.

'Uncle Eddie', as we called King Edward, also came to Berlin in 1909, and together with other schoolchildren I had to line Berlin's Unter den Linden boulevard. Each of us was given a little Union Jack to wave and we had to stand in icy cold weather in the gaps between the columns of Prussian footguards. Big fires were lit to keep everyone warm. Eventually, the open landau drawn by six horses and carrying the two monarchs appeared in the centre arch of the Brandenburg Gate, preceded and followed by the Sovereign's escort of the Garde du Corps.

The rotund Edward was in the full military uniform of a German general and sat alongside Wilhelm, who was dressed as a general of the British Army. There were uncle and nephew together. Each had a psychological chip on his shoulder and whilst they sat together in apparent friendship they were silently calling each other 'arch-intriguer' or 'arch-schemer'!

The main stumbling block in their discussions was the question of the ratio of British to German warships. One can fully understand why Edward refused to agree to a proportion of sixteen to ten instead of the former ratio of twenty-two to ten, as this would not have been in line with his secret, overall plan. According to this, the role assigned to the Royal Navy in the event of war would be to impose a blockade upon Germany. Russia and France would have to provide the overwhelming land forces, together with Britain's few divisions, and the British Navy would 'rule the waves', thus reducing Germany's war potential to almost nil and starving her population into submission.

Nothing good came out of the ensuing conferences. Finally, Wilhelm flatly refused to be dictated to regarding the size of the German Navy and the rift between the two men deepened and widened. The British press described Wilhelm as arrogant and a 'sabre-rattler'. This impression deepened after he had declared that to one of Edward's closest associates that if Britain insisted on war then Germany would be ready.

The German people, moreover, would not have forgiven their Kaiser if he had neglected to 'keep his powder dry' and his army on alert. This he did. In fact, frequently and unexpectedly he would give orders to rouse a regiment or even a whole division. He would appear in the middle of the night to see for himself that his orders had been carried out. Woe betide any contingent commander whose every man and gun were not in proper order. The Kaiser's own railway train was constantly ready to move at a moment's notice to wherever Wilhelm wanted to go.

The German people were no political idiots either. On the contrary, they were only too glad to have a good night's sleep, safe in the knowledge that there were reliable watch-dogs who would protect their lives, homes and way of life. They also read their newspapers, which informed them about the intrigues of the German-baiting President Poincaré, who in 1913 had been elected under the slogan 'Poincaré-la-guerre' ['the-war']. All political parties in the *Reichstag*, including the

Social Democrats, had voted for the upkeep of an army of 800,000 against a French one of almost equal strength and a Russian of 1.4 million men, not counting the French colonial and the Russian Siberian forces.

The German army consisted entirely of conscripts. With the exception of the officers and a handful of technical instructors, they were just civilians in uniform. They had to serve for two years and were then transferred to the reserve. When their time was up they sang about the blessings of civvy street. Upon leaving the army, whilst they evinced pity for colleagues who remained, they still regretted that they had to discard the Kaiser's uniform. Before that they had their photographs taken with the whole company, battery or squadron and these eventually adorned the walls of the best rooms in their homes. The same kind of pictures could or can still be found in many French and British homes. They were hardly exclusive to 'militaristic' Germany.

That said, German soldiers were very proud to wear the Kaiser's uniform. Their ranks were kept free of antisocial elements such as those with a criminal record, and people with the slightest taint on their character were only enlisted as second-class soldiers. The latter were not allowed to wear the national cockades on their helmets or their caps.

The German army was a kind of melting pot where young men from all classes of the population met and had to adjust themselves to extremely rigid discipline. The aim was to create team spirit. Of course, there were square pegs who did not fit into round holes, or those who let the side down. When a platoon or group consisting of eight soldiers and a corporal were punished because one of them had disgraced his comrades, the culprit could expect a midnight hiding from his own room-mates!

In the barracks, the life of a soldier was not exactly what one would call soft. He had to sleep on an iron bunk with bare boards covered by a bag filled with straw. He had to learn how to keep himself, his uniform and his equipment spotlessly clean. 'Spit and polish' or 'bull' was writ large. In later life a working-class man who had served his two years in the army was looked upon as a most desirable husband and many employers gave him preference because of his neatness and reliability. The pay of a German infantryman was one penny and three farthings per day and out of this he had to buy all his cleaning materials.

A few thousand young men, mostly university graduates or undergraduates, had the privilege of serving only one year in the ranks provided they possessed the necessary certificates of higher education. Not only did they receive no pay, they had to buy their own uniforms and had to hire their helmets, backpacks and even weapons. These were the future officers of the reserve and during their own year's service they had to attend special courses in tactics and in the training of platoons and companies.

On one day of the year, the Kaiser's birthday, the officers of the reserve were entitled to appear in public in the full splendour of their gold-braided uniforms with shining helmets on their heads. Special celebrations were held in schools. When some of our teachers turned up in their uniforms we children were awestruck and admired them tremendously, even though their tunics smelled strongly of mothballs.

The whole *Reich* celebrated Wilhelm's birthday with countless festivities. Every town was illuminated with thousands of wax candles in the shops and in the windows of the ordinary citizens. Big military parades took place and afterwards the soldiers frequented the *Kneipen*, or pubs, sometimes leading to unpleasant results – the above supportive comments about military discipline notwithstanding! Along Unter den Linden the crowds cried 'Hurrah!' as the Kaiser passed in an elegant open equipage drawn by fast-trotting greys. His sole guard, a *Jäger* [huntsman] with the imperial crown on his lapels and wearing a kind of bowler hat with green cockerel feathers waving in the breeze, sat high up next to the coachman. As the carriage approached, the soldiers at the Brandenburg Gate rushed out and presented arms.

At other times, we saw the Kaiser fashionably dressed in frock-coat and top-hat, strolling along the shopping centres accompanied only by one of his sons or an aide-de-camp. There was never an attempt on his life, as so often with the rulers of other countries. He frequented the smart hotels or restaurants for a drink or an informal meal with some of his many personal friends, including poets like the Count of Eulenburg, Jewish shipping magnates such as Albert Ballin, actors, painters and scientists. On his initiative, the Kaiser Wilhelm Institutes were founded and large modern buildings were lavishly appointed with the most up-to-date research equipment. Many Nobel Prize winners worked there, and a great number of postgraduate students and scholars from all parts of the world were proud to be admitted to these temples of science.

In memory of his British mother, in 1906 he inaugurated the German Academy for Postgraduate Medical Studies, the Empress Frederick House in Berlin. Twenty years later, I was proud to be appointed surgeon-in-charge of one of the departments there. The Kaiser generously subsidized royal theatres and opera houses all over Prussia from his own pocket. Berlin alone had one royal theatre and two royal opera houses in addition to a municipal one. All of these had first class, permanent and well-paid resident companies. Furthermore, Wilhelm funded the production of plays and operas themselves at his own expense.

In 1897 Wilhelm founded the Kaiser Frederick Museum in memory of his father. This became a major gallery housing one of the best collections of old masters in the world. He gave a great part of his own picture collection to the German nation. Quite often, the Kaiser could be seen on his own at the gallery mingling with visitors, admiring and studying the masterpieces. Like his wife, the Empress Auguste Victoria, he was deeply religious and contributed freely to the building and maintenance costs of houses of God, irrespective of denomination. From his own factory in Cadinen, Western Prussia he gave valuable majolicas to churches and synagogues and attended Catholic, Protestant and Jewish religious services. As with his ancestor Frederick the Great, his principle was that everyone in his realm should have complete freedom to worship God in his own way.

In the student holidays I often visited the Prussian State Library, one of the largest in the world. In its huge reading-room, crowded with students and scholars of many nationalities sat the Kaiser, surrounded by volumes of thick books, which he read with intense concentration, making notes on large sheets of paper. After several hours he would leave. Out of curiosity, I went to his desk to discover what kind of books the Kaiser had studied. They concerned Hittite art. The attendant told me that the library often had to send cases of books concerning ancient culture and medieval European history to the imperial palace. Some of these books were so rare and precious that they were not allowed to leave the library, even for Wilhelm himself, so the Kaiser would go on foot in 'mufti' to read them, all by himself.

All of this is in stark contrast to the stereotyped figure of Kaiser Wilhelm existing in the minds of so many foreigners and cropping up with monotonous regularity in prejudiced descriptions of his personality. He is caricatured as a monster in human form, a ruthless tyrant or a grotesque clown masquerading as a modern Caligula.

I cannot remember what the German jingoists – and there were many – wrote about Edward VII. Only much later did I read in the British press that the Kaiser called his uncle 'a fat peacock'. No doubt Wilhelm was an impulsive man with his own ideas, which he expressed perhaps more frequently and forcibly than cautious diplomacy would have dictated. He was extremely versatile, but with all his manifold interests he never lost sight of the dangers which threatened his beloved Germany.

Chapter 2

The Outbreak

Let us now return to the Kaiser's army. I have already tried to describe its composition and the establishment of a sort of privileged class of soldiers who were to be the future officers of the reserve. Medical students had to serve as ordinary soldiers for half a year with the infantry and the other half as medical officers after they had qualified as doctors. They were allowed to choose a regiment which was garrisoned in a university town and they could continue their studies provided the hours of military duty permitted.

I received an official letter in February 1914. With no mincing of words, I was ordered bluntly to appear at garrison headquarters at the unearthly hour of seven o'clock in the morning for my medical examination as a prospective soldier in the Kaiser's army. They kept me waiting for at least three hours in a draughty corridor. I began to wonder whether this was to see whether I had resistance to the common cold. Then I had to undress completely and enter a chilly room, in the middle of which was painted a white circle, inside which I had to step. A medical officer examined me with a wooden stethoscope – the modern ones with rubber tubes and earpieces were not yet in use. He made me read letters, tested my eyes for colour-blindness, my ears for deafness and my water for albumen and sugar.

Some three weeks later another letter arrived. This one informed me that I was medically fit and asked me to state which regiment I wished to enter for my compulsory military service. As a medical student at Freiburg University, my choice was clear. Freiburg was an old and famous university, tucked away in the pine-covered hills of the Black Forest. I had lived there during the happiest years of my youth and I had become a 'student prince' there, proud to wear the coloured cap of my college, where I had fought duels with sabre and rapier. [Duelling was popular between university students among the German and Austrian upper classes in the nineteenth and early twentieth centuries. Sharp-edged swords were used and a facial duelling scar became something of a badge of honour.]

Shortly afterwards I received my call-up papers. These ordered me to report on 1 April 1914 in 'a clean state and free of vermin' at the barracks of Freiburg Infantry Regiment No 113. I had just arrived at the barracks when a fierce-looking sergeant took charge of me and some other recruits. We had to take off our civilian clothes and put on uniforms – blue tunics with red collars, red cuffs, black trousers and red stripes. Eight gleaming brass buttons fastened the tunic and three others adorned each cuff. Our helmet, the traditional *Pickelhaube*, consisted of stiff black patent leather with a brass cone on top. At the front, the Prussian Eagle stood proudly, also of brass. The whole ensemble looked resplendent in every respect!

I was taken to a room already occupied by seven old sweats. They showed me my bunk, put a brush in my hand, and my first duty as a soldier of His Majesty was to scrub the floor of a barrack room in my university town of Freiburg.

A few days later the new recruits had to assemble on the parade ground in their best uniforms with shining helmets, leather belts and jackboots polished until they shone like mirrors. Our superiors gave us ample opportunity to try out the time-honoured formula of lamp-black mixed with lard and spit, applied with a cork and rubbed in with plenty of elbow grease. In front of the battalion drawn up in the square we had to take an oath to the Kaiser. The regimental colours were ceremoniously unfurled and about ten of us, including me, had to step forward. We had to hold up our right hands, touch the richly embroidered silk flag with our left and repeat the words of the oath spoken by the adjutant.

On the barrack square we were initiated into the art of the smart salute for officers, from the oldest general to the youngest corporal. We had to learn traditional parade-ground marching; in other words goose-stepping ad nauseam. Believe me, fifteeen or even ten minutes of goose-stepping equal six hours of route marching.

Our training, however, was focused on the use of weapons at the rifle ranges. I must say that after a few weeks our instructors succeeded in making almost every one of us a first class shot. The beautiful surroundings of Freiburg with its hills, valleys and forests were ideal training-grounds. Night marches and night patrols made us highly efficient in the role we were to play in the near future. When, after long and exhausting route marches, perspiring and covered in dust (in those days the roads were still untarred), we returned to Freiburg, the regimental brass band would meet us and lead us through the streets. We returned often from night exercises at six or seven o'clock in the morning, rousing the citizens from their beauty sleep. They would stare out of their windows at us with no great enthusiasm. On one occasion a formal complaint about the noise of the band was made to the CO of our regiment, with the result that we sang our marching songs instead, as this was our long-established right.

We marked off on our calendars the remaining days of our active service. At the end of July 1914 we celebrated the birthday of the honorary colonel of our regiment, the Grand Duke of Baden. We paraded in the main square of Freiburg. The whole regiment turned out in shining helmets, blue tunics and spotless white trousers. This was followed in the evening by theatrical performances and a dance, and no soldier was admitted unless he was accompanied by a damsel. I brought a particularly pretty girl and at once had a small skirmish with one of the young officers of my company, who tried to pinch her for himself. This altercation over, the captain played the piano and the major danced with a private who had disguised himself as a Black Forest highland maiden.

A few days later we began studying maps for the manoeuvres of our division fixed for September, near to the family seat of the Hohenzollerns [some 50 km south of Stuttgart]. We had heard the story of the brutal assassination of the Crown Prince of Austria in the darkest corner of the Balkans but took very little interest in that fateful event.

I can state truthfully that even a few days before the outbreak of war neither I nor any of the soldiers or officers of my regiment had the faintest idea of the awful disaster about to befall us and the world; agreed, our views of the political situation were very limited and politics were never discussed amongst regular soldiers.

However, we read in the papers that the Kaiser was on holiday on board his yacht near the North Cape and that a considerable number of the British Navy were guests of the German fleet at the Kiel Regatta. They were anchored right in the Bay of Kiel, the German naval base.

All this certainly did not look like an orchestrated and planned war of aggression on the part of Germany. She just drifted into the greatest catastrophe in the history of mankind. What a difference to the demonic machinations of Hitler twenty-five years later!

Suddenly a rumour went round of a rapid deterioration in the political situation. We heard that Jean Jaurès, the French socialist leader and proponent of a Franco-German rapprochement, had been assassinated. Poincaré's government feared that riots would break out and they planned to have thousands of potential supporters of Jaurès's ideas arrested but alas not a single Frenchman raised his voice in protest . . . they were all for *la guerre de revanche* and cried out hysterically in one voice '*À Berlin! À Berlin*'. Andrè Maurois describes the joyous scenes in France when at last the 'war of revenge' started.

In Germany, extra copies of the newspapers were printed – there was no radio – and a state of emergency was declared. This was followed the next day by the proclamation of general mobilization. Reservists arrived within hours. Huge arsenals of weapons and ammunition were opened up and long lines of men in field-grey uniforms emerged. We also put on our battledress and camouflaged our shining helmets with grey covers bearing the number of our regiment. The barracks were abuzz with feverish activity. From their gates, well-formed columns of soldiers armed to the teeth, marched to strategically important points. Tales were told of spies and sabotage. I remember hearing one story of a young girl being beaten up by a hysterical mob. She had aroused suspicion by picking flowers on a railway embankment. People believed anything. There were even tales of French cars carrying gold bars to Russia, and so precautions were taken to intercept them.

Our knapsacks were packed in accordance with army regulations. Greatcoats were folded with our groundsheets on top of them, billycans were attached to the backs of our knapsacks and iron rations were doled out. On the barrack square were large grindstones on which we sharpened our bayonets and then each man had to fill his ammunition pouches with ninety rounds.

The night before our departure our company commander spoke to us. He explained that the assassination of the Austrian Crown Prince had been the culmination of long-brewing unrest. Our ally Austria had sent an ultimatum to Serbia. This was to demand punishment for the murderer and his behind-the-scenes collaborators, the 'Black Hand', which was an ultra-nationalistic organization.

Russia claimed that Serbia, as a Slavic state, belonged to her sphere of interest. She had mobilized her armies after the arch-intriguer Poincaré had visited and pledged France's backing in case of war. The Kaiser had sent his brother to Tsar Nicholas II. He had tried personally, though unsuccessfully, to persuade Nicholas to withdraw his mobilization order. However, Russian armies had already invaded eastern Germany. France had also mobilized her troops and had crossed the frontiers into Alsace, where many of our comrades came from.

Thus our Fatherland had not only been encircled but actually attacked from the east and from the west. As events proved, our captain was not far wrong. The menacing attitude of the Tsar's Russia of 1914 towards every nation which, rightly or wrongly, threatened a country which Russia considered as belonging to her orbit certainly bears some similarity to the attitude of the Soviet Union of today [written in 1964].

It took more than two days for our regiment to mobilize fully. At two o'clock in the morning on 4 August the companies and battalions assembled by torch light. Our company commander inspected his men, each carrying 75 lb of equipment. It was still dark and there were hardly any people about when Regiment 113, 3,000 men strong, marched out of Freiburg along a road leading to the south-west. We marched silently and were not in the least enthusiastic. My knapsack, rifle, bayonet, spade and bulging ammunition pouches were almost unbearably heavy. The sun rose and the heat soon became stifling: August 1914 was an exceptionally hot month. Clouds of dust stirred up by thousands of hobnailed boots enveloped us and made breathing difficult. Sweat ran down our faces. The only relief we were allowed was to open the top button of our thick uniforms. After a few days we crossed the Rhine over a pontoon bridge, where the Grand Duke of Baden, the honorary colonel of our regiment, stood with his entourage.

We had hardly crossed into Alsace when we entered a huge forest, the Hardtwald. These woods stretched for mile after mile. Soon the trees swallowed us up with their dense undergrowth but the companies, battalions, regiments and brigades kept together in good formation. We halted and were ordered to lie down but to remain absolutely silent. Not a sound was to be made; nobody was allowed to leave the cover of the trees and the few men who were sent out to fetch water from the wells or the scattered houses had to take off their helmets and tunics and go in shirtsleeves, so as not to betray the presence of German troops.

We were informed that the town of Mulhouse, or as we call it, Mülhausen, had been occupied by a French army corps. After a 'battle' against two squadrons of German light cavalry, the French were celebrating their first victory. From our outposts on the fringe of the forest we could clearly hear the French horns or clarions playing the *Meurthe et Moselle* and the *Marseillaise* – a big victory parade was in progress.

About two thousand feet above the tree-tops a solitary French aircraft circled round and round. However, those aboard the 'plane did not hear or see us. Hence, they did not drop the newly invented sharp steel darts, about a foot long and so heavy that they would easily penetrate a man or a horse. Even so, we had to stand up and lean against the trees because an upright man offered a much smaller target than one who lay flat on his face. Later, these darts were of course replaced by bombs but they were often thrown overboard by the handful or armload in those days. They would descend noiselessly to bury themselves deep in the ground if they did not hit a man or a horse. They were frequently found to be deadly weapons.

There we lay motionless and I conceived the idea of starting a diary – the source material for this book. I had a short pencil but no writing-paper except my army pay book. Strictly against regulations, I used this booklet to start my notes. Later, I wrote down my impressions and observations on scraps of writing-paper, food wrappings and children's exercise books which I found in deserted French schools. I sent all these home and my mother kept them for me. The tiny pay book, like myself, miraculously survived the war. A few years ago I found it amongst old papers and I cherish it as one of my most precious war relics.

The forest we were in nearly reached as far as Mülhausen itself, but between it and the houses were cornfields, the crop ready for harvest and almost five feet high. On the night of 19 August the order came to attack the town. We crept in single file with no spoken commands through about three hundred yards of cornfields. Suddenly we were in Mülhausen. The French were so cocksure that they had not even posted sentries at the approaches to the town. In the streets and houses we found drunken or sleeping soldiers, who put up their hands meekly in surrender. However, in another part of the town, our sister regiment No 114 from Constance met fierce resistance from Alpine troops and suffered heavy losses.

As we went through the town we saw that every wall was plastered with posters which the French had brought with them ready printed in gay colours. They proclaimed '*la victoire et la gloire de l'armée française*', which had come as 'liberators of the suppressed and enslaved town'. The Mülhausers themselves apparently did not feel enslaved; they tore down the French posters everywhere, hung out German flags and greeted us in the most friendly way possible.

The French 7th Army Corps, or rather its remnants, retreated so fast towards the fortress of Belfort that we virtually had to run after them right up to the guns of the forts. At first we found heaps and heaps of French army blankets, greatcoats, black canvas knapsacks by the thousand, belts with full ammunition pouches and then finally French soldiers themselves. They were footsore and completely exhausted. Certainly the defenders of Verdun were of a different calibre!

So the first phase of Plan No 17 of the French general staff had come to nought and Général Dubail was sacked. We found a map all neatly marked up with the different stages of the planned advance towards the Rhine, over its bridges and into southern Germany, in the possession of a French colonel. The French had already crossed the Franco-German frontier before any German soldier had set foot on Belgian soil.

During mopping-up operations I went with a patrol to within 150 yards of the Swiss frontier and I could see clearly the Swiss soldiers blocking the road.

Later, we were billeted in Altkirch, a town of about four thousand people. We lay exhausted on bales of cloth in a weaving-mill and fell asleep. Suddenly, we were roused by furious small-arms fire. A German sentry had challenged a moving light and then fired at it, his bullets hitting a wall next to another sentry, who fired back. Thus two German companies were attacking each other wildly and all because a midwife, called to help at a delivery, was carrying a lamp in her hand.

We were relieved by formations of the reserve army and by regiments still wearing their blue and red uniforms. Some were even wearing the uniforms of postmen, with helmets and rifles dating back to the Franco-

Prussian war of 1870□1. My division, a regular one, was ordered to board a train at a railway station near the Swiss frontier; forty-eight men or six horses to each cattle truck.

For those who have never had occasion to travel in a cattle truck, let alone for a long distance, I should explain that there were three classes of travel. Wooden boards were fitted from side to side in first class. The soldiers had to sit tightly packed on them for days and days on end. Believe me, when one could hardly stretch one's legs, the boards became mighty hard and uncomfortable. Second class had no benches but just a layer or two of clean straw, and third class had bare floor i.e. no straw though with cow manure instead.

There was no light. Those who happened to sit, crouch or lie away from the doors could neither read nor write . . . after all, cattle on their way to the slaughterhouse did not need light, neither did the victims of the Nazis thirty years later, when they were herded, eighty or more to a wagon, into hermetically sealed trucks to be gassed at Auschwitz or Majdanek.

There were, of course, no lavatories. When, for one reason or another, the train juddered to a halt, often on top of a steep embankment, those needing to answer a call of nature jumped out and started to relieve themselves. However, nobody ever knew for just how long the train would stop, and often without further warning it would start to move again. Anyone caught in a compromising position had to hastily pull up his trousers, run like crazy and jump back into the truck for fear of being left behind!

There was no heating either and in winter we would be frozen stiff. As a result, many preferred to travel with the horses in their wagons and I remember vividly a journey through Romania when I slept right next to my horse. These intelligent animals were always careful and never trod on you.

As per regulations we were fed at eight-hour intervals, even though this was sometimes in the middle of the night. The fare was invariably the same type of brew ladled out of huge kettles. It comprised a kind of soup with noodles as broad and flat as tapeworms, with pieces of cow meat as tough as leather.

Just before the first journey on board our luxury train, a torrential downpour soaked us all to the skin and we did not get dry until we arrived in Lorraine, west of Strasbourg.

As for communication in the media, Maréchal Joffre, the French generalissimo, had imposed tight censorship. No journalist, politician or even minister was allowed into the fighting zone. Prime Minister Poincaré himself complained that he was being kept completely in the dark about the movements of the French armies. So the attention of the world and especially that of Britain was focused almost exclusively on the northern part of the long front line, namely Belgium. Nobody was aware that another French army group, working to Foch's Strategic Plan 17, had tried to break through the Sixth German Army, which was under the command of the Crown Prince of Bavaria. To motivate the French troops, the idea was to get to Berlin by crossing the Rhine near Mainz. The aim was to drive to the Rhine and to cut off the German right wing from behind. When this failed, another French commander, Général de Castelnau met his Waterloo and was 'sent to Limoges', i.e. was dismissed.

The French attack ground to a halt near Sarreburg. This was due to the fierce resistance of the Bavarians, whose left flank my army corps took a hand in extending and strengthening. We arrived at nightfall. With light drizzle falling, we were led into a field in front of a wood and ordered to dig shallow defence trenches. There was incessant infantry and artillery fire from our right. At dawn we melted into the forest behind us and waited. Patrols were sent forward and exchanged a few shots with French cavalry. Night came and we continued with our digging. In the early morning of 23 August we attacked in the direction of Luneville-Baccarat.

The padre gave all us soldiers absolution in front of a makeshift altar in a field near a village. Then a bugle call rang out and the French let loose at us with everything they had, firing from cottage windows and a cemetery wall. All the glories of our regiment – the elegant trimmings of the officers' uniforms and the splendid colours □ were ripped and torn in the heat of battle. Ten yards from where I was standing my battalion commander received a fatal shot to the head. Two of his young sons also lost their lives on that ghastly day.

We reached a shallow gravel pit, where we paused. A tall lieutenant came to me with blood running from his head. I bandaged him with his field dressings, which were immediately drenched through with his blood because it is very difficult to stop bleeding from a head wound. A shell splinter tore a soldier's knee wide open. He cried out in agony, 'My knee, my knee!', but I could do nothing for him apart from applying a field dressing, which was far too small and narrow over the gushing knee wound.

We crawled out of our pit towards the Rhine-Marne Canal. There, our regiment or what was left of it had assembled, out of range of rifle and machine-gun fire but still within reach of the French field guns. Night fell and on the dark battlefield red lights appeared going to and fro – horse-drawn ambulances and stretcher-bearers.

When we reopened our attack at daybreak on the same spot as the day before, there lay our dead brothers in arms, including the soldier with the dreadful knee injury. He died holding a small gold crucifix in his hands.

At the start of the hostilities the French wore their brightly-coloured uniforms of blue tunics and red trousers. Now their dead lay on the field of battle, giving every appearance of a mass of poppies intermingled with cornflowers.

We marched without rest or pause towards the little town of Baccarat, famous for its glassworks. The place was almost completely deserted. In one of the houses we found eggs, butter, sugar and flour. It did not take long before we made a giant omelette, which we ate with jam. We received permission to sleep in the houses but were forbidden to undress. We still slept like logs.

However, at about six in the morning the alarm sounded and we raced to a parapet facing a road and the River Meurthe. Incoming machine-gun fire killed some of our men but we could not tell where it was coming from. Suddenly a sergeant spotted flashes coming out of the clock tower of a church on the opposite side of the river and next to a rather wide bridge. Apparently, as we slept during the night, the French had crawled up inside the church tower with a machine gun. The plan had been to force us to keep our heads down whilst their infantry brigade attacked us – Mülhausen in reverse.

We concentrated our fire on the spot where we thought the machine gun was sited, but with no result. More men were killed or wounded. Then a German field gun came up and it brought down the machine gun and its crew with a direct hit. This was just in time, because a second or two later a tightly packed formation of French infantry came out from behind the church and tried to rush the bridge. We fired like mad into the densely grouped enemy formation. It seemed that they were surprised to find us ready for them; they stopped, and as quickly as they had come they ran away and took shelter in the church and the houses.

After a while, a young officer of my company, the son of a well known baker in Freiburg, was sent out to ascertain whether the enemy was still there. By this time the bridge was strewn with fallen Frenchmen. He made it halfway across before being fired upon and falling severely wounded in the middle of the French casualties. We could see all this from a distance of less than fifty yards. All of a sudden a French captain, also wounded, turned round, drew his revolver and shot our lieutenant through the head. A cold fury gripped us, and a German corporal ran out and dispatched the Frenchman with his rifle butt. When the skirmish was over, we buried our dead comrades in the middle of a little square in front of the church of Baccarat.

Now we pursued the retreating army of Maréchal Joffre over fields, across rivers and through woods. My company was part of the tip of the spearhead of the advancing troops. About half a mile in front of us was a patrol of twenty men under the command of a sergeant. Without firing a shot, they had entered a village and taken the mayor prisoner. He assured them there were no French soldiers in the place. They moved on and our company followed. In the middle of the market place we halted, took off our backpacks and billycans and started to queue for food from our mobile field kitchens.

The villagers were staring at us. However, they disappeared suddenly and this was a signal for rifle fire to break out from many of the surrounding houses. Several of our soldiers were killed, amongst them the cook and his mate. We stormed the houses from which the fire had been coming. The fusillade had stopped and yet in the houses we found only innocent looking men in the customary dark blue blouses worn by peasants. We also found a number of French army rifles, still warm from their recent use. Of course, we arrested the men.

In the meantime, our advance patrol had heard the firing, turned round and was returning to the village, when they saw about thirty cyclists racing along the road to the next village. Our soldiers fired at them, brought some of them down and captured the rest, including the mayor who had just assured them that his village was free of French troops. However, each one of the cyclists carried a French army rifle and wore a military tunic under his blue blouse. I saw them being marched away to be court-martialled and most probably executed. Such is war.

After this and many similar incidents the German high command ordered the taking of hostages; usually the mayor and other prominent citizens of the community. They had to be kept until the field security police took over from the fighting men. It happened, especially in Belgium, that despite this precaution sniping at German troops continued and so the hostages were then shot. However, I knew how it felt to be fired on from behind by snipers and understood the rage into which the soldiers were driven when they saw their comrades killed right and left by men disguising themselves as non-combatants. I wonder what the excitable Belgians or French would have done under similar circumstances but they did not have the opportunity, as not a square foot of German soil had been occupied by them except in Upper Alsace, a piece of land about the size of Monaco, bordering Switzerland and right under the muzzles of the heavy guns of the fortress of Belfort.

If we delve into history, however, we find that the methods of the French against the guerillas who helped Wellington in Spain were most savage. These irregulars were sent to the French galleys, where they perished. In Prussia during the Napoleonic wars in 1809 the French shot the officers of a fully uniformed regiment, the Schill's Hussars, for operating behind their lines.

I do not believe a word of the tales of orgies deliberately organized to spur on German soldiers into looting, getting drunk to release their inhibitions to reach a state of uncontrolled excitement. The discipline in the Kaiser's army (I emphasize the *Kaiser*'s army to differentiate it from Hitler's) was exemplary. Our soldiers were subjected to the most drastic penalties for misbehaviour, and we considered ourselves the élite of German manhood.

Only recently I heard a British airman say that whenever he saw burning villages from the air he knew that German cavalry had been there. My own experiences from the ground were just the opposite. Quite often we advanced behind a cavalry screen and then when we entered a place we usually found written in chalk, '*Gute Leute, bitte schönen*' (good people live here, please treat them kindly) and signed '*3/Uhl 7*', which stood for 3 Squadron, Uhlan Regiment 7.

Stories of alleged German atrocities spread far and wide amongst the French population. When we entered one small town the mayor met us with his red, white and blue sash around his middle. With tears in his eyes he begged our company commander to order us not to cut off the hands of the children. We had never heard such bloody rubbish! By the way, nobody ever saw a single child whose hands had been cut off □ quite apart from the medical fact that hacking off a hand without immediate and effective treatment would undoubtedly lead to the death of the child in a few minutes. However, the myth had served to create an image of German cruelty, and myths have a tendency to become facts in people's minds. It has been said that truth is the first casualty of war. Even the Americans fell for this clumsy lie to induce their people into buying Liberty Bonds. On one of their posters they showed a German soldier dragging off a child, presumably to cut off its hands, and the caption read 'Remember Belgium'.

Later in the war, when Germany was starving and could not afford to waste a single ounce of fat, regulations were issued that the fat of fallen or slaughtered animals must be put to the best possible use. Egged on by a high-ranking officer of the Imperial General Staff, certain sections of the British press, as soon as they got wind of these orders, restyled the German abattoirs as factories where fat from the bodies of dead enemy soldiers was extracted to make soap, glycerine or pig food. According to these tales, the bodies were collected from the battlefield, wired together in threes and sent to the factories.

These lies deliberately played on British sentimentality; in particular, the sentimentality of women, who imagined thousands of little children languishing pathetically without hands, or the bodies of their loved ones being cut up in soap factories and thrown to the pigs piecemeal. Despite this, many credulous fools believed such vile allegations and volunteered to go to the carnage of the battlefield for reasons which they had not even grasped. Honestly, what concern was the whole struggle for the average Briton, whose country was never in danger? Whose was the quarrel and whose would be the gain?

However, in spite of this grossly unfair, mendacious and malicious propaganda, the stream of volunteers soon dried up and Britain had to introduce conscription for large parts of the battle front. This was quite contrary to her original intention. We laughed when we first heard about the tissue of lies spread by the enemy propaganda machine. Later we became furious and regarded them as utterly unfair, mean and intended to besmirch our honour. It was an effort to bolster flagging morale, but the propaganda resulted in hatred which in reality did not exist between our two nations. German centres of learning had been crowded with British scientists. Now they classed us as savage Huns or Mongolians. By contrast, German soldiers were never guilty of such insults against their British adversaries. They just called them 'Tommies'; the French *poilus* were for us just 'Frenchies' and the Russians 'Ivans' or 'Russkis'. Only for the Italians did we use the derogatory title '*Katzelmachers*', a word which cannot be translated into English but which means makers of little paste figures, especially cats.

During the early days of the war at any rate, I am completely sure that the ordinary Briton was as unaware as the ordinary German of what had caused their countries to fight each other with such cruelty and bitterness. Hatred only sprang up in the civilian populations as losses grew. Such feelings were ignited and fanned by the machinations of journalists and dishonest politicians.

During a short transport stop I met a teacher from my old school, who was an officer in a newly arrived reserve infantry regiment. I heard something from him, for the first time in weeks, about developments in world events. The front-line soldier hardly ever knew what was happening five hundred yards to the left or right of him, and of course at that stage of the war we did not have any newspapers. I hardly believed him when he told me that Britain had entered the war against Germany. The Germans considered the British as kinsmen, cousins, and everything the British did was held in the highest esteem in Germany. Far from hating them, on the contrary we admired them.

This said, admittedly, at the turn of the century there had been anti-British feeling over the Boer War. Germans saw this as another British imperialist attempt to grab even more territory, notably after the discovery of rich gold deposits near Witwatersrand. All this lay in the past, however, and most people had forgotten it.

Many years later, after having been granted British citizenship, I asked an English doctor why he hated the Germans. His answer was that the Prussians wanted to interfere with the British way of life. It is astonishing how well-educated people can utter such ridiculous nonsense. The doctor looked incredulous when I told him that, on the contrary, countless Germans would like to adopt British customs, which they regarded as shining examples of justice and fair play. This was in spite of the behaviour of certain elements of the British people during the Great War.

Had there been a sinister German plot against the British, it would have been child's play to trap their battle fleet when it was anchored in Kiel Harbour shortly before the outbreak of war. French armies had invaded Germany time and time again. Berlin had been occupied by them during the Seven Years' War in the reign of Frederick the Great, and later Napoleon had stood beside the coffin of *Der Alte Fritz* ['Old Fritz', as Frederick the Great was nicknamed] in Potsdam. The Russians with their Panslavic tendencies had always been obsessed by an expansionist spirit.

What on earth did the British have against us? Were they really upset and surprised by Germany's invasion of Belgium? The Imperial General Staff had long foreseen this as inevitable in view of the fact that the French had built a chain of forts and fortresses along their eastern borders (like the Maginot Line which was to be built later). In accordance with the French Plan 17, the purpose of this chain was to lure the German army into French territory and then to annihilate them from behind.

Were the British, on whose empire the sun never set, really envious of industrious Germany who also wanted to have her place in the sun? Hundreds of books have been written on the subject. Many of these contradict each other and we, at least at the time, were in no position to judge the matter one way or the other. My teacher, an historian, sat with me in a ditch at the side of a road along which the endless stream of field-grey soldiers flowed forward, while long columns of ambulances full of wounded travelled in the opposite direction. The schoolmaster was a pacifist at heart but he left me in no doubt that branding the Germans as a warmongering nation out for conquest was a sheer distortion of history.

In the east, huge Russian armies had invaded Germany; in the west, France had attacked her; in the south, beyond the Alps, stood the Italians.

The latter were still undecided, not as to whether but as to when they should dishonour their treaty obligations with Germany and Austria and join the opposition. In the north was the powerful British navy, imposing a tight blockade destined to strangle Germany and to starve her people. If this was not the result of a deliberate policy of *Einkreisung* [encirclement] then Britain did not know what the word meant.

As for us poor footsloggers, what could or should we do? We were merely tiny cogs in a huge war machine and we simply had to obey orders and do our duty and that was that. I shook hands with my old teacher and we said *Auf Wiedersehen* but I never saw him again . . . he was killed a short time later.

So we slogged on living in a coma, as it were. Often we slept while we marched. When the column came to a sudden halt we ran our noses into the billycans of the men in front of us. Our advance was so fast that the horse-drawn supply trains could not keep up and so we went hungry. So hungry, in fact, that we picked raw turnips into which we stuffed coffee beans to try to improve the flavour. The villages we found were usually deserted. Here and there we found cows which were in agony because of their overfull udders. Some of our boys who had been farmhands duly milked them and so at least we had milk for our coffee. The food stores were empty. Occasionally we might find a piece of mouldy bread or some rancid butter, and so the pockets of every dead soldier were searched carefully for food, friend and foe alike.

On one occasion I found the body of a French officer on a hill. He was already in a state of decay but I turned him over and in his satchel was a tin with cocoa and sugar, ready mixed, perhaps by his wife or mother. It tasted wonderful and at the same time provided a means to stop the diarrhoea from which we all suffered. Usually we had nothing to eat except unripe fruit – with predictable results. Before he left Freiburg, the commanding officer of one of our battalions swore that he would only return victorious or not at all. About five weeks later he was back in hospital in Freiburg suffering from severe dysentery!

And so we limped on. We often found wells which had been deliberately contaminated by having the contents of cesspools added to them, whilst dead animals were to be found floating in rivers. Our feet were swollen, blistered and bleeding and we were filthy and unshaven for weeks. During the daytime the merciless sun scorched us and at night we would shiver with cold from about two o'clock in the morning, once the dew started to fall. This was in spite of our greatcoats and groundsheets, which we wrapped around us. Often we would be drenched to the skin by the rain and one night I found myself lying in what had become a small stream with water running down my neck and back. When we came to a halt and the command 'company dismiss' was given, we put our rifles together in pyramids and let ourselves fall down beside them on the hard road without even bothering to take off our helmets or heavy backpacks. Sometimes we slept on the muddy soil of potato fields. If any one of us had harboured any romantic ideas about the nature of war, his illusions would have been shattered in no time.

When we did meet the enemy after such long marches we were often so exhausted that we fell asleep in the middle of battle. On one occasion, we had to cover 42 miles on foot and with empty stomachs in just twenty-four hours. This had to be done in full kit including weapons and ammunition. Soldiers who were overcome by sleep on sentry duty were shot out of hand. For minor offences they were tied to the wheels of the ammunition carts for hours on end.

Men did not dare to fall behind on the march. They had heard rumours of atrocities by French and Belgian *franc-tireurs* [sharpshooters], who allegedly murdered any footsore German they found. There were liars on both sides, however, and some invented or sensationalized stories to make headlines. Many years after the war I read in a British journal about a boy who claimed he had seen a whole bucket full of German eyeballs!

We were moved from one sector of the firing line to another as reinforcements or to stop a gap. On other occasions we came through villages or little towns where there were long rows of stretchers with casualties waiting to be brought to the operating tables. Others had already had limbs amputated or had bandages rounds their heads. Not exactly encouraging sights. We often had to march knee-deep through straw which had been laid in front of houses in which there were cases of tetanus or lock-jaw. The straw was meant to reduce the vibration from artillery or ammunition columns rumbling over the cobblestones of the streets to lessen the awful convulsions of those with that disease. This deadly infection affected at least one per cent of all casualties, because their wounds had become contaminated by the heavily manured soil of the French fields.

Our advance was rapid, though the retreat of the enemy was faster still. All we found were well prepared but undefended positions, which, much to our chagrin, were full of empty tins of French army rations. At one spot we found a whole French battery of four 75mm guns ready to fire, though the post had been abandoned without a shot fired. There was not a man to be seen.

Finally we lost contact. Patrols were sent out with the order to find the elusive enemy. Having risen to the exalted rank of lance corporal [*Gefreiter*], I took a few men and went forward through woods and fields, along ditches, hiding under hedges, avoiding roads and villages. This was the first time I had led a patrol and I was pretty scared. Every bush and tree seemed to hide a Frenchman with his rifle at the ready, and I crawled forward in the half-light only to discover that what I thought were enemy soldiers were just lumps of rock.

Then as luck would have it, we spotted the French infantry and artillery columns marching away from us in the direction of nearby fortresses. I sent off my report with a tolerably accurate sketch. When we returned at night the German outposts fired at us. Because we did not know the password of the day, men of another German regiment mistook us for spies and captured us. However, as we could explain who we were they soon released us and my CO recommended me for the Iron Cross. During the Napoleonic Wars in 1813, Frederick William III of Prussia had created this medal at a time when the Germans fought with the Russians and the British against the French, and it was reintroduced during the Franco-Prussian War of 1870 1. My grandfather won it whilst serving in the footguards with a young subaltern called Hindenburg [later to become Field Marshal, hero of the Great War, President of the post-war German republic from 1925 to 1933 and the man who appointed Hitler as Chancellor].

Maréchal Joffre had sent his armies into battle with the strict order 'Attack, attack!', but now his men were seeking refuge behind the thick walls and heavy guns of the countless forts in the area. On the other hand, the German high command had no intention of letting us take on these formidable obstacles and so our advance slowed down. This gave our supply columns the opportunity to catch up with us and at last we had something to eat. Our ranks had grown thin; many of my fellow soldiers who had marched out with me from Freiburg had been killed or wounded or had fallen ill. We could do with replacements. In fact, we got so many that our company sergeant major was afraid that our mobile kitchen would not be able to cope with them. His fears proved unnecessary, though for tragic reasons.

We were in hilly country not far from a French fort. Sparsely wooded ridges ran parallel to our road and we halted and rested on the side of such a ridge away from the enemy's guns. They opened up on us but the heavy shells could not hit us and landed without exploding, in a morass between our ridge and the next. Foolishly, we clustered together – a whole company. As it happened, I had to answer a call of nature and took myself to a secluded spot about 150 yards away. All of a sudden there was a terrific bang, and the blast of a violent explosion almost knocked me off my feet. A heavy shell had hit one of the few trees around and sent a shower of deadly splinters right into the middle of my company. Forty-two men were killed or wounded as a result. The backpack on which I had laid my head a few moments before was pierced by a large piece of steel which went right through it as if it were a tin of beef. I guessed I was born lucky!

My division had been on active service and was due to be replaced by formations of the reserve. After a series of long route marches we reached a railhead. Here the inevitable cattle trucks carried us in the direction of Mons and Valenciennes, where we got out and marched via Douai into the mining district of Pas-de-Calais. At the beginning of the war we had been fighting along the extreme south of the German lines and now we found ourselves on the northernmost flank. At first not a single enemy soldier was to be seen, but finally a few French patrols on bicycles appeared. We halted near La Bassée and dug trenches. Initially, these were just one-man trenches but after a few days they were joined together. The process accelerated, with huge numbers of men involved, and the lines of trenches soon stretched from the North Sea to Switzerland.

My regiment was shifted back and forth from one position to another. There was a little village called Vermelles, around which we dug our trenches so that they bulged to form a horseshoe into the enemy lines. We were fired on from front and rear and the only road leading to this place was under constant machine-gun and artillery fire. An untenable position. Finally, we received orders to evacuate the stronghold but it was three days before the enemy realized that the trenches and houses were empty. In the meantime, we had gone into another village called Loos. This was soon to become the centre of bitter and furious fighting, where so many British and German boys lost their lives.

At that time, Loos itself was fully inhabited and I found a billet in the house of an old French miner and his wife who were most hospitable to me. There we sat around an iron stove. The old man with arthritic fingers would hold his little grandson on his lap, letting him puff at his old clay pipe, whilst the *grand-mère* also smoked a pipe. They gave me their son's bed. He was a corporal in the French army. I helped them draw water from the pump, carried coal for them and swept the yard. She often said to me, '*Oh, monsieur, la guerre c'est un malheur pour vous, pour nous, pour tout le monde.*' ('The war is a great misfortune for you, for us, for everyone.') It did not take long before shells put an end to this idyll; the people had to leave their homes and the houses were razed to the ground.

Back into the trenches. They were often just a few hundred yards apart and between them was no-man's-land. At night, reconnaissance parties would be sent out. Sometimes in the daytime a little hare would run about, only to be fired at by friend or foe. Occasionally the opposing positions were so close to each other that we occupied one side of a street whilst the enemy held the other. We climbed into lofts and fired into the rooms of houses on the opposite side of the road or flung hand grenades through the empty holes of what had been windows. Part of our trench went right through a cemetery. We cleared out the contents of the family vaults to use them as shelters from the artillery fire though hits from heavy shells hurled coffins and semi-rotted corpses high into the air.

Winter was approaching and it became foggy. One could easily lose one's way in the veritable maze of intersecting trenches, especially at night. One cold night two *poilus* ran right into the arms of our men. They were carrying a large kettle full of delicious-smelling hot rum punch. We put it to good use and let them partake, but only after they had learnt to say '*Bitte schön*' and '*Danke schön*'.

Our food usually arrived at about three o'clock in the morning and the menu consisted invariably of a thick soup with noodles and tough meat. In addition, each man received half a loaf of black rye bread, a piece of sausage and some margarine. The field kitchen usually stood in a shallow glen or small wooded area half a mile or so behind the lines, and here one soldier in eight had to queue with the billycans of his comrades. Often they lost their way to or from the kitchen. Sometimes they would fall into shell-holes or would have to fling themselves to the ground, losing the contents of the billycans, during a burst of artillery fire. Given a choice between losing his life or the food, the soldier would say, 'To hell with the noodle soup!', and so the broth would be off the menu for twenty-four hours. After some months, large canisters were introduced which were strapped to the backs of the men ☐ still for noodle soup, however.

The water from the swampy fields flowed into our trenches. This often meant our standing waist-deep in water for as long as eight to ten days at a time. Lying down or even sitting was out of the question owing to the depth of the water. We tried to alleviate the situation by baling out the water but it immediately rose again from below because the water table was usually only two feet below the surface. Often our boots would be lost in the mud for good. The greatest tragedy was that men themselves, and sometimes the wounded, would drown. They were listed as missing presumed dead.

Then there was the pleasure of playing host to the company of repulsive and often rather aggressive guests – lice and rats. The lice sucked our blood and the rats grew fat munching on the corpses of our fallen soldiers. They used to favour the eyeballs and liver in particular. On one occasion during night patrol I approached something which looked like a body. I saw three or four fairly large black shapes rushing away – rats.

A sentimental girl wrote to me from back home. She said how proud I must be to be allowed to fight for the fatherland and even mentioned the words of Horace, *Dulce et decorum est pro patria mori* ['It is sweet and honourable to die for one's country'.] What utter nonsense! I thought it would be much more important to live for my country. However, this was more easily said than done. Only the night before, our platoon had lost five men whilst they worked to strengthen the barbed wire in front of our trench. These obstacles were desperately needed because the French had brought in troops from Senegal against us. They stalked like leopards across no-man's-land and were real masters at cutting and crawling through barbed wire. We hung tins containing a few stones in them to rattle when anyone tampered with the wire. In spite of this the black soldiers managed to get through to jump at you, stab you or cut your throat. They would come and go noiselessly.

I was on sentry duty on a pitch-black night staring into the emptiness in front of me. My rifle was at the ready and my bayonet fixed. I had to keep my eyes and ears open for two hours, after which I would be relieved. My thoughts wandered to Berlin. I remembered watching the arrival of the splendid carriages at the Royal Opera House in Unter den Linden. The occupants wore full evening dress. The gentlemen wore white tie and tails with silk-lined cloaks around their shoulders, and the ladies were in glittering robes with long white gloves which reached high above their elbows.

Now in the filth and mud of a front-line trench in northern France, I pictured going to a gala performance at the Royal Opera House with my mother and two sisters. They were dressed elegantly and would certainly have to wear those long white gloves. During a spell of leave later, when I actually did accompany them to the Opera, it turned out that not only did they no longer possess white gloves, they could not even buy a pair. Instead, I was cornered and put on a charge by a military policeman (a so-called 'home hero') because my own gloves contravened regulations. Weeks later, when my CO received notification of my crime and was asked to punish me, he laughed heartily and put the piece of paper to proper use.

There I stood, half-frozen with stiff, mud-covered hands. I could hear the rumble of heavy vehicles in the distance behind the French lines mostly likely bringing up more ammunition designed to kill us.

The end of 1914 came nearer. News spread through our ranks that another regiment might be taking over from us, allowing for Christmas festivities behind the lines in rest quarters. Replacements arrived at about three o'clock in the morning and we groped our way through communication trenches waist-deep in icy water. We were wet through and the uniforms froze to our bodies in the bitter cold.

After a two-hour march we reached our accommodation. These were houses blasted by shell-fire, with holes in their roofs and no window panes. We blocked the gaping holes in the window frames as best we could with old rags and straw, some of which we also spread over the cold damp tiles of which the floor was comprised. We took off our uniforms to try to scrape the loam off them. However, they were so caked in mud that they virtually stood upright on their own. Candles were lit and an incredible amount of mail distributed. Chocolate, cheese and bacon parcels were opened and I received a small box of my favourite cigars from my parents.

Christmas Eve is the festival for family reunion in Germany and the troops looked forward optimistically to a relatively quiet one. Typically nostalgic songs were sung about homes and families far away in the Black Forest and the gathering took on an atmosphere of peace. We kindled fires in the familiar French iron stoves and were just about to have our evening meal – noodle soup, even here – when the alarm was raised. We had to put our sodden uniforms back on, pick up our backpacks, rifles and belts and march back again into the shit.

Someone in the high command had the idea that the French were about to launch an all-out attack on our positions, based on the assumption that the sentimental Germans would relax their vigilance on Christmas Eve. Nothing of the kind happened. However, when we returned behind the lines two days later all my parcels had disappeared, including my cigars and the four pairs of mittens which pupils of the Frieburg girls' schools had knitted for us.

Part II
(1915)

The events of 1915

March	The French plan two offensives on the western front: eastwards from Artois and north from Champagne. The Artois offensive opens at Loos and Lens; the Germans are driven back but send for reinforcements.
22 April	The Germans attack at Ypres. Gas is used for the first time.
2 May	German bombardment against the Russians starts across a 28-mile front at Gorlice-Tarnow in Romania. More divisions are brought up by the Germans from France under General Mackensen but by the time of arrival the Third Russian Army has already abandoned its positions. The Russian retreat slows but counter-attacks meet with little success.
9 May	The German defensive position is smashed by the French, who advance 2.5 miles until the Germans are reinforced. Fighting continues until 15 May with appalling losses to the French. After a brief lull, intense fighting resumes for another four days.
25 September	Double French offensives in Champagne and Artois. They fail to break through though are more successful in Champagne than Artois, despite the fact that Rupprecht only has two divisions in the front line.

28 September	French attack reaches the crest of Vimy Ridge but the weather is against them.
8 October	The German counter-attack is driven back.
4 November	The campaign peters out on all sides. French and German casualties are very high, with little achieved.
29 December	Joffre proposes Somme offensive.

Chapter 3

The Western Front

New Year's Eve 1914 saw us back in the front-line trenches still digging and baling out water. I thought of Sisyphus, the mythical King of Corinth, condemned forever in the underworld to push a huge stone uphill, only to see it roll down again when it reaches the top. We crawled out of our positions to repair the barbed-wire entanglements, and a patrol went out, only to return minus one man. Instead of the church bells of Berlin, the New Year was brought in for us by salvo after salvo of French artillery shells. Quite a number of our chaps did not live to see the dawn on New Year's Day. Still, our noodle soup arrived punctually and the unremitting drudgery continued.

Now the most insane period of the trench warfare set in, with a bloody struggle for every inch of stinking trench. For each advance of a hundred yards, one or two hundred men had to die. Forward positions were lost and retaken in bitter hand-to-hand fighting. I often asked myself how civilized and educated men could hurl themselves at each other like mad dogs, savagely thrusting bayonets into the chests and stomachs of their opponents.

Bombarding a military position with artillery shells, firing at it with machine guns or rifles from a distance, dropping bombs on it from the air, these are all quite impersonal acts. You hardly ever see the enemy face-to-face. It is surely quite a different matter to be in close proximity to him and to try to thrust your bayonet into him or split his skull with the sharpened edge of a spade. This is surely the worst sort of cruelty. It certainly proves that all our much-vaunted cultural achievements are nothing but a thin veneer, which all too easily drops away to reveal barbarians of prehistoric days standing in front of one another. It cannot be said that the Germans' *furor teutonicus* was unique, since the French, the British, the Japanese and all the others behaved in the same way, whatever their achievements in the fields of art and culture. All sense of humane feelings was lost in the heat of battle. The only thought was to kill one's opponent.

A shudder runs down my spine even now when I see, many years later, in a film or on television that recruits are being trained in the same way. They have to run their bayonets into bags filled with hay whilst shouting blood-curdling cries of self-encouragement. I think of all the soldiers (including myself) on the battlefield, who actually had to enact these horrors.

We received an order to storm a strongly fortified French position and rushed across no-man's-land wondering how this would end. Arriving at the enemy position breathless and with our blood up, hand-to-hand fighting began in deadly earnest. In the ensuing melée I looked around just in time to see a French corporal ready to plunge his bayonet into me. As we both had our bayonets at the ready it was clear to me in an instant that this was a case of my having to kill him before he killed me. Frequent sabre duels in Freiburg as a medical student had taught me the importance of swift and decisive action. The next split-second of time seemed to go into slow motion. He lunged at me. Out of pure instinct, I parried his attack and pushed his weapon aside before riposting with my own blade, which I thrust deep into his chest with all my strength. He dropped his rifle and fell. Blood shot out of his mouth. I stood over him for a few seconds and then gave him the *coup de grâce*. After we had taken the enemy position I felt giddy, my knees shook and I began to vomit.

Out of my group of eight soldiers two had been killed; one of them was a Freiburg tram conductor, another an office clerk. Of the survivors, one was a chimney sweep, two were farmers, one a student and another a teacher – all ordinary peace-loving people, who until a few months ago would not have harmed anyone. Now we told each other what we had achieved: one had killed a Frenchman with a pickaxe, another had strangled an officer and a third had crushed the skull of a *poilu* with his rifle butt.

So now we were all murderers. However, it seemed to me that whilst we were all now standing on the brink of insanity I realized that without people such as us wars could not be waged. We had been taught time and again that there is no room for sentimentality on the battlefield and that any soldier who sees his enemy as another human being is a bad soldier. The good soldier knows that it is his duty to kill. Every war is total war, and the words of General Sherman hold true: 'War is cruelty and you cannot refine it.'

Nonetheless, in my mind's eye I saw the convulsions of my victim. Even in death his face showed the agony I had inflicted on him, and his hands were clamped over the wound where I had stabbed him. For a long time afterwards his glassy eyes stared at me in my dreams and I would wake from my nightmare bathed in cold sweat. I can quite understand that after experiences like this men can lose their minds and I later had occasion to see such cases for myself. My thoughts haunted me. However, I tried to reason with myself that it would have been my own fate had I not been quicker than him.

On another occasion, part of my unit's position was taken by the enemy. During the fight over a few hundred yards of swampland I saw a French soldier about to throw a grenade towards my platoon. He saw me and appeared to freeze for a moment. This gave me the brief amount of time I needed to close the gap between us and hit him between the neck and shoulder with the sharp edge of a digging tool which I happened to be holding. In fact, I hit him with such force that he was dead before he hit the ground. However, the tool was buried so deep in his body that I had difficulty extracting it. Realizing how effective this weapon could be, I put it to similar use again soon afterwards on my third victim of hand-to-hand fighting.

As for me, I no longer cared that my uniform was drenched in blood; I had become battle-hardened and so nearer to the ideal of a good soldier. My actions earned me promotion to full corporal [*Unteroffizier*] and the Grand Duke of Baden decorated me with the Military Medal of Merit.

I wondered which aspects of war can turn a so-called bad soldier into a good one. Team spirit, perhaps. Possibly innate fear of what the enemy will do to him. I mused that there is hardly a human being alive who is not consciously or unconsciously afraid of death and over-compensation for this fear in a soldier can degenerate into something we call courage. So fear equals courage; a paradox indeed!

Of course, there are people who have an innate strain of sadism or cruelty in them, or who are so primitive or psychologically underdeveloped that they have yet to grow out of the mental state of wild beasts. This said, we know that a wild animal only kills out of an instinct for self-preservation, either to sustain itself or defend itself; in other words, when it is frightened. Socrates, however, has another explanation. He says that fear of being considered a coward by one's own comrades overrides one's fear of the enemy. Lastly, there is the unexplained impulse of daring, which leads people of all ages to do things which no normal human being would try to do in a sane frame of mind.

In the meantime, a newly formed division of the Kaiser's army had been put together. It comprised entirely new recruits: mostly young students and schoolboy volunteers, who urgently needed officers and NCOs. As our Regiment 113 had a surplus of these a number of us were listed for transfer. One of those listed so disliked the idea of leaving his old regiment and pals that he reported sick and so I was given the short straw. By then I had acquired a fatalistic attitude and bade farewell to my friends and left. After all, most of the faces around me were now new because the old ones had vanished. I heard later that the man who reported sick had been killed by a sniper's bullet soon after I left.

After something of an odyssey we arrived at a suburb of Lille called La Madelaine, probably named after Mary Magdalene, the so-called sinner of the New Testament 'out of whom went seven devils'. I hardly ever saw so many 'ladies-in-waiting' standing around on street corners. Often whole streets had been converted into brothels. In fact, my own billet was in a 'house of joy', though my presence as a German corporal in such an establishment threw a spanner in the works. However, this was not my fault.

Finally the Kaiser's new division arrived. It was armed entirely with Russian rifles and guns, which had been picked up on the battlefields of eastern Germany. Our first task was to weld the rookie recruits into some kind of fighting unit. We taught them how to distinguish shell-fire from mortar-fire, how to feign death, flatten themselves into the ground and throw grenades so that they exploded a split-second before they hit the ground – all the tricks a seasoned campaigner had learnt by trial and error. After two weeks we moved back into the front-line trenches.

I had to go to regimental HQ with a message. Whist waiting for a reply in a sort of ante-room at a dugout, I could not help overhearing a heated argument between our colonel and the divisional commander.

They were in the next 'room', separated from me only by a screen of thin sacking.

Our colonel was strongly opposed to an order from his superior for us to launch a full-frontal assault over a flat piece of ground in broad daylight. We were being asked to take a brickworks about four hundred yards in front of our trenches and not far from the La Bassée canal. In the colonel's opinion this cluster of baked and piled-up bricks was not of the slightest strategic interest or tactical value. Furthermore, it was bristling with machine guns, heavily fortified and protected by dense barbed-wire entanglements. He pointed out that his regiment consisted almost entirely of young recruits and that were this madness to go ahead, it would be necessary to soften up the enemy position with heavy artillery fire before any attack.

The Lieutenant General reminded the Colonel that artillery cover was absolutely impossible as our guns were almost out of ammunition – three shells left for every gun, to be exact. Germany herself had run out of ammunition due to lack of gunpowder, and the new factories to extract nitrogen from the air were only just about to start production.

The debate went on and on, though no one wins an argument with a lieutenant general unless he happens to be a full general himself. In this case, the General was also the Corps Commander and he was desperate to win the Iron Cross, First Class. Finally it was decided that the only chance would be a surprise attack against the enemy and to cover the ground to the target so quickly that there would not be enough time for the enemy machine-gunners to man their posts.

Thus on two consecutive nights patrols were sent out to reconnoitre the terrain. This achieved nothing except that my company lost nine men; we were also sure that several of our chaps had been taken prisoner. So even the element of surprise had been removed. We could also see through our field-glasses that the enemy had made everything ready to give us a hot reception. In fact, he had used the hours of darkness to strengthen his position. By now the brass-hats must have realized that even though the so-cleverly thought out surprise attack would now be impossible, they were still so obsessed with their bright idea that they insisted on carrying it out.

With a sense of impending doom we cut zigzag lines into our own barbed-wire entanglements for us to filter through and white tape was put in place to guide us. We went over the top at noon. After barely a hundred yards we ran into a virtually impenetrable wall of rifle and machine-gun bullets, whistling and whining all around us. My Company Commander had his face shot away; another man started yelling and whimpering with his hands clamped to his stomach as his intestines protruded through his fingers. Then he staggered forward and his head hit the ground. A young man cried out for his mother as bright blood spurted out from his face.

The order to 'take cover, lie flat on the ground' was shouted. I flung myself into a shallow shell-hole, half filled with muddy water. There were four other chaps, of whom two were wounded. The water slowly turned red as the moaning and screaming of the wounded grew louder. The enemy machine-gunners sat on top of the brickworks and let rip as soon as anything moved. Nobody moved an inch; we were sitting ducks. After some time a few tried to run back to the relative safety of our own trenches but they could not find the gaps in our own wire and were soon killed □ caught like flies in a spider's web.

Meanwhile, the enemy's observers had alerted their artillery batteries. They opened up. This had the effect of flinging legs, arms, heads and whole bodies high into the air. The ground shook from the explosions and large chunks of brown earth rained down on us. We heard the hiss of jagged, red-hot shell splinters going over our heads and pressed our faces into the mud as deeply as we could.

Then, as if someone had waved a magic wand, the rifle, machine-gun and artillery fire suddenly stopped. An eerie silence fell upon the bloody 'field of honour'. What the hell was going on? Were they about to launch a counter-attack? With gallows humour, one of our lads asked whether they were about to serve refreshments. Finally, we dared to peep over the edge of our hole and could hardly believe our eyes when we saw a British soldier dressed in khaki emerging from among the piles of bricks. Furthermore, he was waving a white flag with a red cross and was being followed by stretcher-bearers, who slowly walked over to us. They laid the wounded on the stretchers and carried them towards our trenches. Almost paralyzed by fear and still numb with shock, we stood up and helped them. By now our own stretcher-bearers had taken over and the British returned to their brick heaps. A short while later a kind of truce was arranged for the armies to collect their dead. Had this act of mercy not taken place everyone knew that the stench would be unbearable, quite apart from myriad flies which might bring epidemics.

The whole episode had lasted barely half an hour though it seemed like an eternity for us. The bulletin issued by the German army merely reported a 'flare-up of trench warfare on the Western Front'. However, no fewer than 960 young men had been killed, and all this just to gratify the whim of an irresponsible and over-ambitious general. One statistically minded soul calculated that the combined French and Prussian losses during the three days of battles of Viouille, Mars-la-Tour and Rezouville in 1870 were fewer than those we suffered that horrible afternoon in just a few minutes. I do not know whether the brass-hat got his Iron Cross, but we quipped that the German dead got their crosses all right.

Having lost so many men and having had so many others cut to pieces, my regiment was withdrawn from the front line. New cannon fodder was sent up to replenish our ranks. We marched to the rear, companies of 230 men reduced to 50 and led by sergeants as all the officers were dead.

We came to a railhead, where trains were standing ready to transport us; the cattle trucks once again. Before we boarded we had to cover up everything which might reveal to any prying eyes which regiment we belonged to. The numbers and signs painted on the sides of the baggage carts were scraped off, the field-grey covers of our helmets bearing our regimental number were turned inside out and our shoulder-straps were folded so that the numbers could not be seen. Elaborate ruses were carried out to deceive the enemy. Whole divisions were carried deep into Germany before being returned to the Western Front a few days later in different railway carriages.

A constant puzzle for the British and French intelligence services was that many German units wore the same numbers on their shoulder-straps even though they belonged to different regiments. For example, there would be an original regiment, then reservists, followed by the *Landwehr* (mostly old reservists or recently trained men) and finally the *Landsturm* (soldiers too old for the front line). The latter would be entrusted with guarding the communication lines or stretches of the front which were of minor importance.

We steamed on towards Germany. The train stopped at the frontier and we had to leave our wagons . . . for delousing. It was a case of having to take off our uniforms and underwear and putting them in bags of coarse netting, to which we affixed numbers, with identical ones hung round our necks. Then we had to subject ourselves to a kind of sheep-shearing. Fast electrical clippers removed every trace of hair from our heads and bodies, including the beards which many of us had grown. I did not recognize some of my fellow soldiers because I only knew them with their resplendent flowing beards.

Next we had to undergo a kind of sheep-dipping in huge containers full of evil-smelling disinfectant. After this we were marched into another hall and sat down to a meal – more noodle soup. What a sight! A whole battalion of warriors dressed only in their birthday suits with close-cropped scalps. No distinctions were made between officers and other ranks, and the lice did not differentiate between them either. To them, soldiers' blood and officers' blood tasted just the same. They carried the germs of the dreaded spotted fever or typhus, and whole armies had fallen victim to this pestilence. DDT had not yet been invented.

It took about an hour to sterilize our clothes and after they had left the huge autoclaves they were returned to us. Lice-free railway coaches waited for us – no cattle trucks this time – apparently in order to show the German population that their men were not shifted about like animals. We went through the outskirts of Berlin and then via Silesia into Polish Galicia, where we arrived shortly before the battle of Gorlice-Tarnów.

A huge army had been assembled under the command of General Mackensen. We hurled ourselves against the Russian lines. However, before we reached them 'Ivan' had vacated the lines and we found only superbly built fortifications. Had these been stoutly defended they would have cost us rivers of blood to take.

Two regiments, about five thousand men, of German infantry had been sent to strengthen the Austrian lines. We advanced on a broad front, knowing that Austrian troops were supposed to protect our left and right flanks. I write the word 'supposed' because we knew that many Austrian army units were highly unreliable. The majority of the Croats and Serbs in their ranks were illiterate peasants, who had no idea what they were fighting for. Their officers had to be bilingual, because the soldiers only understood their first language. Whenever a battle became really hot they turned round and headed for home. Moreover, the Czechs were often anti-Austrian. In the middle of the night they would raise a white flag and surrender to the Russians. Whole battalions or regiments, such as the Prague House Regiment, joined forces with their former enemies, taking their arms with them.

We did not come across a single Russian soldier for miles and miles. We thought our troubles were over, at least on this part of the front. Our artillery had been diverted to another sector and so we were on our own. We stopped on the edge of a huge cabbage field, from which we could overlook the flat countryside. To avoid exposing our heads to enemy fire we dug shallow furrows in the earth and used the soil to make small mounds in front. We could also use the earth as cover from which to fire at the enemy ourselves.

In the distance was a large forest but there was not a soul to be seen. Suddenly, a dense-packed formation of brown-clad Russian infantry emerged from the wood and ran nearer and nearer. Rifle bullets began to hit our earth mounds. Our platoon commanders shouted, 'Range six hundred yards, fire!'

The Russians stormed on undaunted. Through our field-glasses we saw cavalry formations on our flanks and thought they were probably Cossacks on their typically small horses. Apparently our Austrian friends had deserted us and left our flanks uncovered. For their part, the Russians were attempting to catch the whole lot of us in a pincer movement.

We changed our sights to three hundred yards and fired as rapidly as we could. Our rifles became red hot. The water in our machine-gun cooling systems boiled, and many went out of action. Then our ammunition ran out. In the meantime, the brown-clad soldier-hordes kept on coming. At a hundred and fifty yards we fixed bayonets and made ready for hand-to-hand fighting. Suddenly the Russian steamroller came to a halt and they began to dig in. This came as a relief. We hardly had any ammunition left to fire at them, and I was down to the last round in my magazine.

Night fell and we received orders to extract ourselves as best we could from the Russian grip. Orders were given to stick cabbages on top of the low earth mounds, don our soft field caps which we carried in our back-packs and to put our Prussian *Pickelhauben* (helmets) on top of the cabbages. A few of our cavalrymen stayed behind to harass the *moujiks* (Russian infantry) with their light machine guns. They did this until morning, at which point they galloped away.

As for us, during the night we crawled back behind our own lines and then marched off. We would have loved to have seen the faces of the 'Russkis' when they discovered that they had been firing at cabbages instead of the dreaded 'Germanskis'. Mind you, the Russians had wheel-mounted machine guns, too, and they knew how to use them.

In any case, we had great admiration for the sheer courage of the Russian infantrymen, as we knew how it felt to be on the receiving end of machine-gun and rifle fire. In my opinion, the Russian foot-soldier was the best we had encountered up to that point in time; fearless, tough, resolute and with an utter contempt for death. However, just like the German generals, the Russian generals obviously did not realize how easily the soft-skinned bodies of their soldiers could be pierced by steel or the lead of bullets. With their vast numbers, they regarded life as expendable. Later we were told that only every third Russian soldier carried a rifle and that the others had to wait until they could pick one up from a wounded or dead comrade. We could testify with our own eyes that they collected rifles from the battlefield and still stormed on against us.

Back we went to France in the cattle trucks. There we manned positions in Artois, between Bapaume and Arras along the most westerly part of the front line. It was hilly country and ideal for the mole-like work of undermining the enemy trenches. The French *mineurs* scraped and shovelled underneath our dugouts and the German sappers counter-mined to destroy those of the French. As long as we could hear the hammering we knew that the enemy was not yet ready to blow us sky-high.

Our trenches ran through the tiny hamlet of Serre, opposite Hébuterne. Serre consisted of about ten houses, but when I visited it after the war I counted no fewer than five French and British war cemeteries in its immediate neighbourhood.

At the time, a fellow soldier with whom I was friendly acquired some bottles of wine and invited me and a few others to celebrate his birthday with him in the cellar of a house shot to pieces by artillery fire. I got plastered and went to sleep in my bunk full of unthreshed straw. The bunk was infested with mice, who became most indignant when I turned from side to side. In fact, their squeaking would often wake me up. This time, however, I slept soundly with my blanket over my head; so soundly, in fact, that I did not hear the arrival of our CO and some other high-ranking officers who were making a visit to our den in the small hours of the morning. I had become a full sergeant in charge of a platoon by then and should have greeted them. Fortunately, when the General saw me fast asleep my friend had the presence of mind to tell him that I was a casualty waiting for an ambulance to take me behind the lines for treatment. 'His Excellency' left the dugout on tiptoe so as not to disturb me.

I met my friend again some nineteen years later, by which time I was a British doctor. We had not seen each other at all since that moment and I learnt that he had been posted away before I woke up that morning.

A few days later I was wounded for real.

Chapter 4

Surgeon Probationer

My luck had been holding until now but in Serre they got me! While inspecting a listening-post in front of our lines a heavy shell exploded almost on top of me and, according to my fellow soldiers, sent me hurtling through the air. I only recovered consciousness several hours later, when I was being dragged into the dubious safety of a slit-trench. I was wrapped in a groundsheet and carried through the trenches to the advanced dressing station. After nightfall, they took me behind the lines on top of a *panje* cart, named from the Polish word *pan*, meaning master. These were low, wooden, high-wheeled vehicles, without springs and drawn by small but very strong Siberian horses. Thousands of them had been captured from the Russians and brought over to the Western Front. They were certainly not fit for 'masters', but good enough for us.

I was perched on a stretcher across the wagon with three other casualties. Although we were more or less securely tied on, when we went over roads riddled with shell-holes in the middle of a moonless night, all four of us did have to hold on tight to avoid being thrown off.

Finally we reached the casualty clearing station at Achiet-le-Grand. This was a tiny village later to be the scene of fierce fighting. One by one we were taken into the operating theatre. The theatre itself was lit by candles and acetylene lamps. I can still remember the surgeon in his blood-splattered apron bending over me to operate on the wounds in my groin and buttocks.

We were then taken to lie in long rows on reasonably clean and fairly comfortable straw-filled sacks in the local church. The Sergeant Major rebuked me roughly for not lying to attention when the Medical Officer passed my bed. According to regulations, patients were to lie with their arms outstretched stiffly over the blankets as if down their trouser seams, like rookie recruits on the parade ground. I could not care less, as every bone in my bone hurt and I was bruised all over.

After a few days in the draughty and unfriendly church I was taken by motor-ambulance – a recently introduced contraption – with three other soldiers stacked one above the other, to Bapaume and from there by train to St Quentin. We were taken to the main surgical block at the Palais de Justice, where we were undressed and thoroughly washed by female nurses. Alas for us young guns so full of *joie de vivre* who had not seen a German woman for almost a year, they were unapproachable nuns.

I was X-rayed by one of the first such machines in army use. After the doctors had found out that my bones and vital organs were all right, even though a shell splinter had passed through my pelvis, I was treated as a convalescent. My wounds healed so quickly that they did not even send me back to Germany.

Any day now I expected that my commission as an infantry officer would come through. This was known as a 'one-way express ticket to eternity'. Front-line subalterns had a life expectancy of weeks or days – bad risks, indeed, which no life assurance company would have touched with a bargepole.

However, at the clerk's office someone discovered that I was a senior medical student. I was swiftly transferred to the Medical Corps as a second lieutenant, or surgeon probationer as they were known in the British Royal Navy. Whilst army officers could be quickly churned out by the hundred, army doctors were a different matter, even though they possessed as little medical knowledge as I did then.

Strangely, large parts of the Western Front were more or less dormant at that time. Especially opposite the French lines, exhausted German divisions would be sent to recuperate and to be re-equipped. Legend had it that near Rheims a large bell was hung up to be rung to wake the soldiers up in case peace broke out. The same applied to positions in Flanders, where we were confronted by the remnants of the Belgian Army. There were only captured Russian guns at our disposal, and it was said that birds had made their nests in the muzzles. In the meantime, the locals lived peacefully in their houses next to the gun emplacements.

Newly appointed surgeon probationers were given the opportunity to make the best use of any relatively quiet times at the front for further medical education, by being posted to large hospitals behind the lines. In St Quentin with its thousands of beds, real university classes were run by army consultants, all of them famous professors. Classes were given in clinical medicine, surgery and many other specialities. In addition, we had to be on duty as housemen, and I was attached to the main surgical block at the Palais de Justice. There, in the former court rooms (the *salles de pas perdus*) was a huge hall with hundreds of rows of beds, often occupied by three different patients in one day.

Quite often we would be ordered to move any patients who could be safely transported to the rear. They would be loaded into ambulance trains and taken either to Germany or to special reception hospitals like the one at Le Cateau. The latter is well known to students of the Great War as a result of the bloody encounter there between the British Expeditionary Force's 'Old Contemptibles' and the German Army on 26 August 1914. Le Cateau housed more than 10,000 casualties (Germans and POWs) in large textile factories which had been emptied of their machinery.

After two hours or so a new wave of wounded would arrive at the Palais de Justice. They were brought to us in motor-ambulances pulling up to three two-wheeled trailers behind them, each carrying three more men. Of necessity, these trailers had to be light-weight but so were their springs. A journey on top of them over pot-holed roads was no joy ride for the wounded, many of whom had broken bones which had only been set provisionally and were not yet in plaster of Paris.

With their full cargoes of moaning and aching bodies, these trailer-trains were clearly marked with large red crosses. However, this did not stop the occasional air-attack – not by the British but by the French, as a rule. They often showed no respect for the sign of mercy, as we shall see later.

We got busy, changed bandages as necessary, and the same evening the casualties would leave again by hospital train to make room for the next load. We had to write case-notes for each patient detailing their types of wounds and the treatment they had been given. This was necessary to let the doctors back in Germany know what they were dealing with. Using indelible pencils, we sketched the position of fractured bones on the patients' plaster of Paris, because the X-rays (exclusively on glass plates at the time) would often break, get lost or be sent to one hospital while the patient arrived at another.

In the Palais de Justice we treated the more serious cases. Here they lay with bullets in their lungs, missing eyes, jaws or limbs or having been shot through the kidneys or testicles. During the day they would often be treated by internationally famous surgeons. For example, my boss was the Professor of Surgery at Istanbul. However, at night I would be on my own.

Our hospital orderly was a Franciscan monk called Brother Ludovicus and he would call me to various cases. One man was having a secondary haemorrhage from the stump of his amputated leg, another was choking from where his throat was swelling after being pierced by a piece of steel, a third was in pain from not being able to empty his bladder and needed a catheter. Brother Ludovicus showed me how to perform this often tricky procedure.

Frequently, a soldier with a seemingly innocent wound would experience a sudden rise in body temperature. This would be the symptom of the dreaded gas-gangrene. The soldier's life would depend upon immediately opening up the tissues surrounding the wound and then the application of hydrogen peroxide. The alternative was to amputate. However, we had no antibiotics, sulpha drugs or ability to give blood transfusions.

During my ward-rounds I would often have to call for the Father Superior, Professor Raymond Dreiling, to administer the last rites to a dying man. Some were no more than teenagers, who would cry for their mothers. Professor Dreiling was in charge of the nuns and monks and was also a doctor of divinity, philosophy, law and medicine.

He was a man full of worldly knowledge, in no way confined to the narrow life of a monastery. We would often end our duties back in the officers' room, at which point he would invariably produce a bottle of wine from under his flowing brown robes. We talked over the day's, or rather the night's, events, and the discussion would turn to the utter futility of war. He too was a pacifist at heart and we both condemned the useless slaughter of men in the prime of life. He reminded me that wars had been fought since time immemorial and that the Holy Book was full of stories of bloody fighting between various peoples and tribes.

I remarked that war was the antithesis of love and that the arrival of Christ's brotherly love should have prevailed. Instead, look what happened. One war after another was launched in the name of God . . . but which one, God, Allah or Jehovah? Weren't the crusaders sent out by the Pope, i.e. Christ's representative, to recapture the Holy Land from the infidel? Yet who were the infidels and who the believers? What about the Thirty Years War in the seventeenth century which reduced the German population from sixteen to four million □ and all this for religious conviction? Perhaps there were other more sinister motives behind all this. Now there were priests of all denominations in all armies who implored the Almighty to help their own side, and the Almighty was at a loss whom to favour. All we had to do was to walk through the wards and to see the mess we were in! What about the Sixth Commandment, 'Thou shalt not kill'? Every German soldier had the inscription '*Gott mit uns*' [God with us] on the buckle of the belt holding his ammunition pouches, hand-grenades and bayonet. Making light of this, the Tommies quipped, 'We got mittens too'!

We sat and discussed the abyss into which mankind had fallen. Sheer blasphemy was being preached from the pulpits by men dedicated to the fostering of Christ's gospel of brotherly love.

Sick prisoners of war were being kept in wooden huts and large tents surrounded by barbed wire and attached to our hospital. I had to look after them. My main assistant was a captured French male nurse, who never stopped telling me about his training school, the Hôtel de Dieu, the famous hospital in Paris. When this highly efficient man was repatriated, in accordance with the Geneva Convention, I regretted it very much. His replacement arrived. This time it was a Tommy POW from St Thomas' Hospital in London.

Two of my patients complained of severe toothache. They were Scottish Highlanders and were sent to the dentist under escort by an elderly bearded soldier. They absconded on the way. Good luck to them, I thought, but a few hours later they reappeared, handcuffed and under the stern gaze of two sturdy military policemen. Their kilts had given them away.

A rather odd situation developed in one of the huts when I met a relatively high-ranking Russian officer. He saluted me smartly and told me that he had been sent to help us in the hospital. It turned out that he was a first class surgeon from Riga who had been captured in East Prussia. He spoke perfect German because of his background in one of the formerly German Baltic provinces and he proved a great asset. This was not only because of his skills and knowledge but also because he could speak to the many Russian prisoners of war who were brought to us. They worked in their tens of thousands on the roads behind the lines and were usually in the most deplorable physical condition.

This was an odd situation because even though I was a mere medical student, my word was law with any officer, however high-ranking, from another country's army. My German army officer status meant that I outranked him and even had to guard him, complete with long sword, when taking him to our fortnightly clinical demonstrations. Any soldiers we met saluted smartly – they probably thought he was a high-ranking Bulgarian officer.

Furthermore, our own medics were astonished when a Russian officer stood up and spoke in German on some of the points which Bier, the famous professor of surgery from Berlin and inventor of spinal anesthesia, made about his new method of extracting small shell splinters from the brains of wounded soldiers. After enlarging a hole in the skull, he introduced specially shaped metal applicators into the immediate area of the shell splinter. Guided by X-ray apparatus, a huge iron block would be lowered by pulleys until it touched the appliance. The electric current was switched on. This magnetized the five hundred pound block which was then raised again. Everyone watched to see whether the small piece of shrapnel would also be drawn from the wound. Most were not. In fact, many soldiers died from meningitis or were subsequently paralyzed from the resultant severe lesions in their brains.

One day I was on duty as MO when an old French labourer came in. He wore baggy trousers, and the stubble on his face was half an inch long. Puffing hard, he produced a scrap of paper on which Surgeon Vice Admiral Bier had scribbled a few words in pencil ordering his admission. Bier had met him on the road and been fascinated by a monstrous goitre, which was pressing hard on his windpipe and causing his breathlessness. So this Frenchman was put in a ward alongside wounded German soldiers. After various preliminary tests and examinations he was operated on by Germany's premier surgeon, assisted by the famous Danzig surgeon Professor Barth and by me – all in the operating theatre of a German hospital of war.

In the case of the Frenchman, I was given the opportunity of watching these two masters at work. I saw for myself first-hand how they handled delicate tissues with all the skill only first class surgeons possess. They operated under local anesthesia and hardly a single drop of blood was lost during almost two hours of strenuous work. The patient recovered quickly and left the hospital after three weeks. He was full of praise for the 'Huns'. His goitre, however, was later exhibited in the Museum of Pathology at Berlin University.

My 'subordinate' Russian surgeon explained to me why he had repeatedly refused to be repatriated. The conditions in Latvia, Estonia and Lithuania (all three former German states) had become unbearable. This was especially so under the policy of Russification, and many members of the intelligentsia had emigrated, if able to do so. He hated the Muscovites and was even of the opinion that they had precipitated the war by mobilizing their armies days before Austria had declared a general mobilization. He thought that the bellicose clique surrounding the Tsar had found the war a very welcome way of diverting the attention of the oppressed classes from their plight in life. He described the conditions behind the Russian lines in vivid terms. Russian medical services were virtually non-existent and hardly any of the so-called medical officers were actually qualified doctors. Instead, many were just barber-surgeons like those in the Napoleonic wars, i.e. people who had acquired a crude knowledge of how to amputate an arm or a leg. This was anathema to the German army and I am sure also to the British and French.

He told me that Russian hospital equipment was incredibly primitive and that on the rare occasions when there were any trained surgeons to be found there were no instruments. The chaos was unbelievable. Bandages, drugs and suture materials would be kept in three separate locations miles apart from one another. Badly wounded soldiers would be left to die as they were considered to be of no further use and would only prove to be a burden. There was a 'couldn't care less' attitude among the high-ups. The life of the ordinary soldier counted for nothing; there were so many of them.

The *moujiks* went into battle with a stoic fatalism. Gradually, though, they developed a class-consciousness, which in his opinion would lead to rebellion. This rebellion would be not only against the ruling classes or *boyars* but also against the *kulaks* or landowners, who until recently were able to sell the souls of their farm labourers. The time was ripe for revolution. Only rigid discipline, often including corporal punishment by the officers and NCOs, held the ranks together. How true his predictions proved to be! As far as surgery was concerned, the administration of an anesthetic was largely considered to be a luxury reserved for officers. Other ranks would be given a bullet to bite on.

Admittedly, our methods of giving anesthetic were also rather primitive. It was usually administered by an orderly or by a nun, as in our hospital. Sister Angelica taught me how to put a man under, the easy way. Today's complicated equipment, blood transfusions, pulse registration, blood pressure measurement or electro-cardiographs with visual read-outs, were all unknown at that time. We just dripped ether on to a mask until the victim went blue in the face, stopped breathing or started vomiting.

When the patient did come round after his ordeal he would often use filthy language, sing obscene songs and tell appallingly dirty jokes. This was all the more embarrassing when the theatre sister was a royal princess, as was often the case where I was working at the time. I watched closely on one occasion but she did not even blush, either because she did not understand the joke or perhaps because she had already heard it.

Patients with infectious diseases occupied a large boarding school or *lycée*, which was previously the British HQ during the battle of Mons. The British field telephones and wiring system we found were put to good use for inter-hospital communication.

One night when I was on duty several cases with cholera arrived. In line with orders, I immediately informed the consultant physician Professor Kraus from the University of Berlin, the army bacteriologist and the head of the pathology department. They could not agree on the diagnosis so they decided to put the patients into quarantine, together with three nursing sisters and my humble self. For six days our food was handed to us on long poles borrowed for the purpose from a local bakery. In the end the cholera turned out to be a harmless form of dysentery. For me it was some consolation that the nurses were not nuns but had come from a Berlin hospital.

It was another of my arduous duties to act as a *locum tenens* to the medical officer inspecting prostitutes working with the soldiers behind the lines. Every woman caught for soliciting and picked up by the military police had to be put in an official brothel. There they had to be inspected for venereal disease on a twice-weekly basis.

All this was in accordance with German law. Under the regulations, all prostitutes had to be registered with the police and were obliged to report every third day at police headquarters for examination by a doctor specializing in sexual health. If a prostitute were found to be infected with a contagious disease, she would be taken immediately to a police hospital for compulsory treatment. Admittedly, however, this was not very successful with the ineffective drugs available. There was no cure in those days for some 85 per cent of the inmates, who had to be discharged in the end, healthy or not. So they were a constant source of infection. Furthermore, the illusion of effective medical care created a false sense of security for male clients, who were under the impression that the police ensured that only healthy girls worked the streets.

If the police surgeons found no acute infection they put date-stamps in the girls' registration books. It was then the duty of every policeman to check these books and if a girl were caught soliciting without a valid stamp in her book, she would be sent to prison. Later it became generally recognized that such treatment was beneath human dignity. Furthermore, it became acknowledged that it would only make the women sink lower in life and end up as criminals. In 1927 the *Reichstag* unanimously passed an Act doing away with the compulsory registration, examination and treatment of prostitutes, which was just a farce after all.

In those days, however, as it was also the MO's duty to look after the general health of these girls, I went nearly every day into the 'houses of joy' and became the confidant of the priestesses of Venus. I learnt that one of them fell in love with one of the doctors. In order to win his favour she revealed to him the existence of a widespread spy ring.

It happened that soldiers of all ages would become drunk and start to boast of their deeds here and there. They often saw in a girl not only a means of sexual satisfaction but also a kind of mother or wife, in whom they could confide. She could listen patiently and sympathetically, egging them on to tell more, not only about their past but also what they expected to do in the near future. Combining these bits and pieces of information, the enemy's intelligence services could put two and two together to gain valuable hints about troop movements, reinforcements or the aggregation of whole armies. With this in mind, German counter-intelligence put up posters in the brothels warning visitors to keep their mouths shut.

The military police kept a sharp eye on brothel inmates and freelance prostitutes. In fact, they kept under surveillance everyone they contacted who might have received useful information. We MOs also received carefully worded instructions to report any suspicious-looking behaviour. Our main duty as members of the army medical corps, however, was to combat VD. During business hours our corps orderly had to inspect every visitor and give him a disinfectant injection when he left.

Elaborate precautions against these diseases were given to the soldiers. If he wished, every man going on leave or being sent behind our lines could receive a small box containing three different kinds of antiseptic. However, in spite of the incarceration of prostitutes, observation of their clients and distribution of drugs free of charge, the number of soldiers and officers infected with VD was alarming. The medical corps set up special *Ritterschlösser* [knights' castles] for them. These were places where they would be treated and kept under a kind of house arrest. Their diet was even more frugal than that of the average German soldier. The head of the medical services at general HQ confided in us that there were many 'knights' who were already cured but had deliberately re-infected themselves to keep away from front-line service.

By no means all German soldiers were heroes. Some invented numerous tricks to ensure they were sent behind the lines. A favourite one was to complain of stomach pains. The MO would, of course, find no trace of any real gastric trouble but when he inspected the patient's mouth he often found the man had no teeth left. He would send him back to the dentist, who would give him a set of dentures. In no time, the dentures would be broken and the whole business would start again. Finally, it was decided to make dentures out of aluminium alloy, which did not break so easily.

St Quentin was not only a hospital town but also the administration centre for the Kaiser's Second Army. It possessed a rather nice theatre, where German artistes performed for the troops. There were bookshops, libraries and also the editorial offices of an army newspaper. In the larger towns behind the lines German restaurants were established. Although still in range of ordinary field artillery, in Peronne on the River Somme Bavarian beer cellars sold Munich beer and fried sausages, served by waitresses in traditional costumes. The war was bearable here. Suddenly, though, I got orders to take up a post as officer in charge of an ambulance train whose doctor had fallen ill. I arrived in Sedan after a long journey and finally the train rolled in full of sick and wounded soldiers. They were covered with a layer of chalk from the earth of the Champagne district and were filthy and lice-ridden.

The train's crew consisted of the CO, i.e. me, a twenty-two-year-old medical student, and about twenty-five orderlies. The main section of the train comprised some twenty inter-connecting carriages each holding twelve beds, so 240 beds in all. In addition, there were a number of special coaches for the less seriously wounded, cases of mental illness and also for wounded prisoners of war. Furthermore, there were carriages for the orderlies and for myself, a kitchen wagon and another for stores.

It was a very long train. There were telephones between my 'office' and each of the coaches, and these telephones were operated from a kind of switchboard, allowing the MO to be called to wherever he was needed. To help me find my way in the middle of the night in particular, there were printed maps with a layout of the train. These showed every bed and seat in the carriages and the different diseases or wounds of the patients were shown by coloured flags, stuck with pins on to the squares.

We never knew what our destinations would be or how long our journeys would take. Thus we had to be prepared for all eventualities and had to have ample supplies of food, drugs and bandages.

Sometimes in the middle of the night, when I was asleep in my bunk, I could feel that the train was being shunted and was moving on. Similarly, in daytime, a locomotive and one or two railwaymen to work the handbrakes would appear, and we would start to travel. Once in Rethel in northern France I went for a drink in the Officers' Mess and when I returned, after about an hour, the train had disappeared. The stationmaster had gone off duty and the new one had no idea where my train had been taken. Only after 'phoning in all directions did he find out where it had gone. How to get there? The answer was for him to put a spare locomotive from the station at my disposal. We raced along in it until we overtook the fugitive train, which finally regained its commanding officer.

I would quite often see lice crawling out from underneath the plaster of Paris covering a broken leg or watch maggots emerging from under a bandage. It was most likely that flies had laid their eggs in open wounds while the men were lying for days on the battlefield. However, these highly unpleasant creatures acted as scavengers and the wounds looked fresh and clean.

We were shifted to and fro. Only the names of the railway stations through which we passed gave us an indication as to the direction in which we were travelling. We would often be shunted into sidings fully laden with wounded to give priority for troop or ammunition trains to pass. It would then fall to me to change blood- or pus-soaked bandages or even to operate in emergency cases.

At Nesle station on the River Somme about 150 wounded British prisoners of war were brought to my train under escort. The Tommies were rather surprised when a German nursing sister broke through the cordon and began embracing and kissing them. This was quite out of keeping with their idea of treatment by the 'Huns'. What they did not know was that this was Daisy, daughter of the British Earl De La Warr. She was also the wife of the German Prince of Pless, a close friend of the Kaiser's. In the end, the Commander of the Guards intervened and Daisy left.

There was hardly a journey on which we did not have to take wounded or sick prisoners of war behind the lines. One fact frequently puzzled me. This was that wounded British prisoners of war were almost desperate in their efforts to avoid being placed in the same compartment as Indian or black troops. After all, they all wore the same uniform. Perhaps, I thought, these British men sensed what an incredible lack of understanding it had shown to bring over to Europe hundreds of thousands of the Empire's Asian and African subjects, who now saw with their own eyes how their white masters destroyed themselves. Only many years later, after I had settled in England, did it dawn on me that such behaviour on the part of white British troops might have something to do with what we now call the colour bar.

The prisoners were usually escorted by elderly soldiers armed with antiquated rifles and put in coaches with specially secured windows. Enemy officers had to be guarded by German officers – we were fighting a gentleman's war. Often the escorting officers were going on leave or had other assignments in Germany and so arrangements were made accordingly.

One day a British pilot officer was brought to the train. He had been shot down and wounded and was accompanied by a young officer of the Imperial Foot Guards. This British airman was a most unpleasant, arrogant and swashbuckling type. He seemed to have an inexhaustible supply of swear words, and the Greek and Trojan heroes of Homer's *Iliad* would have learned a thing or two from him. The orderly in charge of the coach came to me and suggested putting this man into the wagon reserved for mental cases.

When I arrived on the scene I witnessed what was about to become a case of fisticuffs between the British officer and his German escort. The British airman referred to the Kaiser in the most abusive language as the instigator of this bloody war, whereupon the Prussian, who had also been educated at Eton, asked him which Kaiser he had in mind. Perhaps he meant the Russian Kaiser, the Tsar who had mobilized his armies before anyone else, the Austrian Kaiser, the French dictator Poincaré or maybe the Indian Kaiser [King George V of England, who was also Emperor of India, or *Kaiser-i-Hind*]? I intervened and told the fighting stags that I was the Kaiser here and what I said stood.

By way of follow-up action, my well trained orderly, who knew what to do in cases of nervous hypertension, handed me a syringe of morphia, which I injected into the British airman's arm. I then gave the German officer a draft of strong brandy. When I returned after about an hour I found both of them snoring peacefully in their respective corners.

Near to the big industrial centre of Charleroi in Belgium there was a large marshalling yard, to which was attached a locomotive repair shop run by German engineers. The whole operation was guarded by a battalion of old soldiers, who were also responsible for the safety of the railway lines. The tracks led to the forward areas and the bridges over the River Sambre.

When my train had returned from a journey it was shunted into the marshalling yard of Marchienne-Zone, together with other ambulance trains. I soon became acquainted with the officers of the veteran guardsmen and the engineers in the workshop. Their haunt was an *estaminet* or café in a nearby village called Montigny-le-Tilleul, and I joined them there for a glass of beer and game of darts. The proprietor was a most obliging fellow and suggested that we form a kind of darts club to play against the local team. The young village locals came and we were quite a happy lot. We were sorry to hear that 'Charles' had to go to hospital or that 'Aristide' had moved to another district and it was unlikely that we would see them again.

However, one day we arrived at our favourite café to find it closed. We were informed that the security police had arrested the landlord because it had been found that his café was a staging-post for Belgians to be smuggled across the Dutch border to join the Belgian army.

Ambulance-train doctors, German engineers and battalion officers had been used ingeniously as cover. Nobody suspected that such activities would be carried out under the very noses of German officers. A British nurse called Edith Cavell was found to be the leader of this underground organization. She was sentenced to death and shot. We discussed the ins and outs of her execution, which was later used to such great effect as anti-German propaganda. It was of course, a political blunder par excellence by the Germans, but what would the British, the Belgians or the chauvinistic French have done in similar circumstances? Answer: they simply shot the beautiful German spy Mata Hari, and that was the end of it.

Christmas was approaching once again. Every member of the Second Army commanded by Prince Rupprecht of Bavaria received a large beer mug from him bearing a facsimile of his signature. I kept this *Seidel* for many years and used it on many occasions. Finally it suffered the fate of all crockery – it broke and was thrown away.

Shortly before the end of December, the ambulance trains in Marchienne-Zone were given orders to evacuate all infectious or mental-disease patients from the hospitals near to the front lines. We were to bring them back to Germany and discharge our sordid loads into specially erected hutted hospitals near Cologne. The trains had to be thoroughly disinfected afterwards and we were shunted into a large railway repair works near Nippes, a suburb of Cologne.

We had to leave our trains and were billeted in third-rate hotels nearby. This was too much for me, and I decided to join my family in Berlin. As the officer in charge of an ambulance train I had whole booklets full of leave vouchers and railway warrants at my disposal. I confess that I forged the signature of a non-existent colonel. I travelled for almost twenty hours in an overcrowded train to my home town, and my mother could hardly believe her eyes when her eldest son turned up on New Year's Eve.

Part III
(1916)

The events of 1916

21 February   German attack under General von Falkenhayn against the French on a 15-mile front at Verdun. By 24 February Germans had advanced 3.5 miles and French were in retreat.

25 February   One German company captures Fort Douaumont.

28 February   French reinforced and halt German advance. By 6 March German attack covers a wider front.

10 April   Germans attack in force south of Douaumont but are repulsed by heavy fire. Advance slows down but on 7 June Fort de Vaux captured.

21 May, 2 June   Minor attacks by Germans have some success at the Somme.

24 June   Preliminary British bombardment at the Somme for seven days, with Germans faring badly.

1 July   The assault at the Somme. In the south the French are successful but the British advance meets with formidable resistance. German machine guns win the day. British suffer huge losses. Heavy German casualties also.

14 July   British take German second position at Bazentin Ridge successfully. Germans rush in reinforcements.

August☐ November	Battle of the Somme continues, with British hoping to wear down German resistance to make renewed assault possible.
27 August	Romania enters the war on the Allied side.
24 October	French hit back at Verdun, recapturing Douaumont and Vaux with heavy losses to Germans.
13 November	At the Somme General Gough wins battle fought on both sides of the River Ancre; British success continues. Bad weather draws offensive to an end. Total losses to Allied and German armies both number over 600,000.
26 November	Von Falkenhayn takes last Romanian stronghold and enters Bucharest on 5 December.
12 December	Peace proposals by Germany but completely unacceptable to Allies.
15 December	German reinforcements brought in at Verdun to meet new French offensive but French continue to regain ground.

Chapter 5

The Trenches of
the Somme

New Year's Day in 1916 in wartime Berlin was a sad one for all of us and for me in particular. My father had died only a few months previously. After much deliberation, my superiors had granted me three days of compassionate leave to go to see him when he was dangerously ill. When I asked for an extension of my leave as his death was imminent, they flatly refused. I had to return to my post with a heavy heart. The powers that be probably feared that the war in the west could not be won without me!

In the meantime, my sisters and my younger brother had gone with friends to Switzerland. However, at the border, one of my sisters was made to strip so that the German border guards could scrub her back with soap and water! She was only twelve years old. The guards did this because they had found out that children had been used to carry secret messages, which had been written on their backs.

When I went to my favourite coffee-house in Berlin, no one from past times was there except the old head waiter. He told me that all of my pals had either been called up or had gone away on war work. He had also heard that several members of our circle had been killed or wounded. One or two had come to visit the old coffee-house and found it deserted, just as I had done. One of my uncles was with a reserve regiment on the German-Danish border, where a landing by the British was expected. Another member of my family had been killed in Russia and a third was in hospital minus a leg.

Even though there was no blackout, the streets were dimly lit or in darkness. Berlin was out of reach of enemy bombers but often the electricity or gas works had to close down for lack of fuel.

Even by the standards of the German climate, the winter of 1916 was very severe. The snow was knee-deep. Whatever their class or profession, everybody had to clear the snow away from the fronts of their houses. Judges, cobblers, actresses or clergymen were all involved in this work. However, when they woke up again the following morning there would be fresh snow, at least as deep as that of the previous day. Inside the houses and flats it was icy cold; there was no coal and central heating did not exist. The city council of Berlin had opened large halls for public use. Mostly elderly people gathered there to warm themselves around the big stoves and to have a dish of hot soup.

The food situation was almost indescribably bad. The first thing I had to do was to go to the food-ration office because without a ration card my mother was unable to buy anything for me. I also had to thank the non-existent colonel, who had signed my leave cards, for a ration book.

Sugar was unobtainable and one even needed coupons to obtain saccharin. If you wanted to eat just one potato in a restaurant you had to give up a coupon. Later on in the war especially, bread was just a powder-like substance of potato peelings and ground turnips mixed with rice flour and sawdust. One had to be careful not to swallow little pieces of wood.

Well, here I was on New Year's Day in my home town of Berlin. In the streets the women wore shabby clothes and dresses which had already been repaired several times. Most of the clothes were black, because they were in mourning. The newspapers were full of notices announcing the deaths of those who had fallen on the field of honour for Kaiser and country. I felt utterly lonely and disappointed. In order to celebrate my arrival my mother had invited some of our friends round to our house. They greeted me warmly but after a while I got sick and tired of answering their constantly repeated questions as to when, where and how I had earned my Iron Cross or how life was in the trenches. They also wanted to know whether the stories they had heard or read about this and that battle were really true or only exaggerations by overenthusiastic journalists.

On a subsequent trip home I got so fed up with all this well-meaning interest that I went to a nearby seaside resort on the Baltic coast out of sheer desire to be left alone. However, when I arrived at the hotel I felt as though I was a ram in the middle of a flock of ewes. Sex-starved females stared at me from all sides. The chambermaids, waitresses and grass-widows all sent little notes to ask whether I would like to join them for dinner . . . just to begin with.

I found my own bed at home too soft and could not sleep. In short, I felt miserable. I heard the same story from almost all my fellow soldiers when they returned from leave. Those who were married told me that the first two or three days home were like heaven. Then all kinds of friction arose. Husband and wife would often drift apart during the years of separation; the husband frequently suspected that the wife had found a lover □ perhaps a highly-paid munitions worker. In the meantime, the poor devil home on leave from the war had to be content with his penny-three-farthings pay, which would not even buy a glass of beer.

Whilst we all dreamed of the bliss of going home on leave, most of us came back disillusioned and were glad to be with our regiment again. We were all sharing the same dangers and had the same kinds of problems which the bloody war kept in store for us.

A telegram arrived informing me that my ambulance train had been disinfected, deloused and repaired. My mother came to see me off at the station. She waved and waved her handkerchief until the train disappeared around the bend in the railway track.

Once in the carriages, the customary war language could be heard again in the overcrowded compartments: the old swearwords, the old catchphrases and the old slogans so well known to all of us were once again bandied around. The atmosphere in the train reverted to what we had been accustomed to during three years in the trenches or on the battlefields.

At the other end of my journey, the crew of my ambulance train turned out to meet me in full strength. My first job was to check out the hundreds of sheets, pillowcases and blankets which had been removed and washed before the disinfection started. This done, and having replenished our larder and stores, we were ready to go back on duty.

After I had made several journeys on the ambulance train, the previous CO turned up fully recovered. As far as age and experience were concerned, of course, he was a man in every respect my senior. My orders were to hand the train and its contents over to him and to report for duty as a regimental MO with a field artillery regiment near to Verdun. Upon arrival, I found an artillery duel in full spate and the air filled with smoke, dust and the whining of shells.

Back at regimental HQ, a telephone message had been received. One of the telegraphists had been taken ill at his observation post at Fort Douamont. He was complaining of severe abdominal pain and was vomiting. There was no choice but for me to leave my post and to go there in person. The French artillery had started firing poison gas shells into the German positions and so as well as my steel helmet, I took a newfangled contraption with me – a gas mask. The mask itself was primitive. It was like a surgeon's mask, and inside it you had to lay a pad of cotton wool soaked in a fluid which was supposed to filter the air you breathed to protect the lungs from the poison. The eyes were left uncovered.

Reaching my patient was easier said than done. On our side, German sappers had dug two deep communication trenches leading up to the hill on top of which the fort was situated. It did not take long before the French gunners found their range. They then proceeded to keep these lines of communication under constant fire. As a result, large sections of the earth to the right and left of the trenches were completely rucked up by the shellfire. The trenches themselves were hit time and again.

I took two stretcher-bearers with me, one of whom knew where to find the observation post. When we finally arrived I found the patient in agony, obviously suffering from acute appendicitis. We carried him into the fort and down one flight of stairs after another. Deep in the middle of the fort and protected by many feet of reinforced concrete, the French had built an operating theatre. We Germans were making good use of it. In fact, there were always two German surgeons on duty there and one of them happened to be from Berlin. They confirmed my diagnosis and started to operate immediately.

During the operation I could feel the whole fort shaking. Heavy shells with delayed action fuses would land and then explode at an indeterminate later time. However, we were safe where we were, and only a few flakes of whitewash fell from the ceiling.

After the operation, I strolled through the fort. Complex engineering was evident and the place boasted a labyrinth of dugouts and sub-chambers. However, the entrance to one of the sub-chambers was bricked up and someone had fixed a plaque to it with the inscription, 'Here lie 1052 German soldiers'; a whole battalion. Apparently, one of them had been smoking during the night while the others were asleep. A carelessly discarded cigarette or match had ignited the barrels of fuel stored there for flame-throwers and these had exploded. Not a single man had survived.

It was always a big problem how to bring wounded or freshly operated-on soldiers to the relative safety of life behind the lines. When enemy wounded were being moved, we observed that on those parts of the front line where we were opposed by British troops, a white flag with a red cross was carried by the enemy through the most forward trench. Our soldiers stopped firing immediately, and the big guns were also kept silent until the red-cross flag disappeared. The British would do the same for us.

We tried a similar procedure here at Verdun. A kind of convoy was formed, with a man walking in front carrying a flag with a red cross, another man in the middle and a third bringing up the rear. However, the French reacted differently. They intensified their artillery fire, with the result that quite a number of our stretcher-bearers were wounded or killed. There seemed to be a difference between British gentlemen and French cavaliers! In the end, we decided to trust our luck at night and to strap our wounded comrades to our backs to bring them to safety.

Burying fallen soldiers was virtually impossible. Trench-digging parties in no-man's-land would come under fire immediately. Again, the best thing to do was to make shallow trenches at night. The bodies were laid as they were, with their uniform and boots left on. However, as the war progressed, orders were issued to remove dead soldiers' boots because leather was becoming scarcer and scarcer in blockaded Germany.

In the forward positions at the front line, dead soldiers were thrown into spare communication trenches, one on top of the other. These open 'graves' were then sealed off with a few sandbags. If the pits were too shallow, our friends the rats would appear from nowhere and burrow tunnels until they reached the corpses. Then the rain would wash away the soil, and quite often one could see a half-eaten hand or foot sticking out of the ground.

Fresh artillery was brought up to the front line and our regiment was withdrawn. Our men had become completely exhausted and the barrels of the guns were so worn that they had become almost unusable.

I was transferred to an infantry regiment a few days before the long-expected British offensive on the Somme. Our job was to strengthen the lines south of Beaumont-Hamel. On 24 June 1916 the British guns opened up. They intensified their fire, in conjunction with massive gas attacks. For seven days and seven nights in a row the ground shook under the constant impact of the shell-fire. In between the bombardments the gas alarms would sound and we could hardly breathe. Our dugouts would crumble, toppling in on top of us, and our positions were razed to the ground.

Again and again we had to dig ourselves out of masses of blackened earth and splintered wooden beams. Very often we would find bodies crushed to pulp and bunks full of suffocated soldiers. The pounding never ceased. Fresh supplies of food or water never reached us. Below the ground, men became hysterical and their fellow soldiers had to knock them out to prevent them from running pell-mell into the deadly hail of shell splinters. Even the rats panicked. They sought refuge in our flimsy shelters, running up the walls, and we had to kill them with our spades.

My first-aid post was in a hollow where the sappers had taken the trouble to dig and build two exits. One of these received a direct it. However, even though we still had the other one we got busy clearing the first – well you never know!

On the morning of 1 July the British gunners switched their artillery fire to our rear position and their armies went over the top in massed formation. They even threw footballs over their parapets and started to run after them because they did not expect anyone on the enemy side to have survived their bombardment. However, German machine-gunners and infantrymen still managed to crawl out of their holes. In fact, it was a kind of relief to be able to come up from the trenches into the smoke-filled air heavy with the smell of cordite. With sunken eyes, faces blackened by fire and uniforms splashed with the blood of their wounded comrades, they started firing furiously.

This intense German fire produced frightful losses on the British side. It was estimated that the British lost at least 14,000 men in the first 10 minutes. Their advance was certainly no more than a mile on our part of the front before the whole mighty offensive ground to a halt. The British and French generals had not yet learned that it was useless to send human beings to run against machine-gun fire, even after a week of so-called 'softening up'.

One of the most difficult tasks which the medical corps had to perform was to bring the casualties from the battlefield back for the attention of the medical officers. It took cold courage to venture out under heavy artillery fire, when everyone else was crouching in a hole. When the wounded soldier had been found, he needed to be laid gently on a groundsheet or some kind of improvised stretcher and then carried carefully through the deadly rain of shells or across treacherous minefields. The stretcher-bearers often had to crawl through barbed-wire entanglements or shell-holes half filled with mud and water. The wounded man would then be dragged back over the field, often under constant machine-gun and rifle fire.

At night, stretcher-parties had to fling themselves flat on the ground when Very lights turned night into day. They would often be mistaken for patrols and fired upon. All of this meant that often the rescuers would themselves be wounded and new attempts had to be made to bring all of the casualties back for medical attention.

On one occasion, a wounded soldier was lying between our trenches and those of the enemy; we could not see him but we could hear his cries for help. Stretcher-bearers were sent out to fetch him under cover of darkness but two of them were wounded and a third was killed. Finally we received strict orders to abandon the first casualty. We heard his cries for another three long days and then there was silence.

Another time, from the entrance to my dugout I saw two of our stretcher-bearers running through what had once been a wood. Now there were only splinters and flame-scorched stumps of trees sticking out of the ground like threatening and accusing fingers. We heard the whine of an incoming heavy artillery shell and flung ourselves down the steps into the comparative safety of our bunker. The big shell exploded with an enormous bang, sending up a mountain of earth, stones and red-hot steel shards.

Over the place where the two men had been a cloud of black smoke hung ominously. We could not see anybody and ran out to try to discover what had happened to them. At first all we found were several pieces of the stretcher. Then after a while we found one man with a bootless foot dangling out of his trousers and blood spurting from his wound. We laid him on a stretcher. I tied a piece of string above the knee of his trouser as a tourniquet to stop the bleeding temporarily. Over the spot on his leg where I knew that the main artery was I put an unopened field dressing to exert extra pressure.

There was no trace of the second man for a long time. Suddenly, one of my orderlies saw half a naked torso impaled on one of the tree stumps. Apparently the shell-blast had cut him into two and hurled one half up so high that it was impossible to take it down. More shells were landing around us and so we had to leave his mangled body to rot away – the torso of a man who had gone out to help his fellow creatures.

Mercifully, the first soldier was still unconscious, and we carried him to our tiny first-aid post. I cut open his trouser leg in order to investigate the wound. The string acting as a tourniquet could not be left in its present position for more than an hour or so without the whole leg below it being in danger of becoming gangrenous. Hence I removed the string and put forceps on the arteries, which began to bleed again. My study of anatomy proved very useful at this point. However, I decided not to risk an emergency amputation and instead put a large wire-splint over the foot and bandaged it as well as I could, leaving the forceps in place.

After nightfall he was carried by his fellow soldiers to the casualty clearing-station. The surgeons there could make a proper job of dealing with the wound. I consoled myself that I had done the best that I could with the meagre resources at my disposal and with my equally meagre levels of skill and experience.

The clearing-station itself was situated near to a road in a forest clearing. It consisted of a number of large tents, one of which was the 'operating theatre' with two tables and two teams of surgeons operating round the clock. The tables were lit by acetylene lamps and the floor was bloodstained duck-boarding laid over the grass.

A few days later, when I asked what had become of my stretcher-bearer patient, they hardly remembered him because they had been so busy with other cases in the meantime. Finally they found out that his foot had been amputated and that he had been taken to a field hospital further to the rear. The sergeant in charge of the operation tent just shrugged his shoulders when I asked for my artery forceps back. I waited until he turned his back before helping myself – only to find out later that I had grabbed two more than I had inserted in the wound of my patient in the first place!

Our stretcher-bearers were often simple folk – dock workers, peasants and wood cutters, who often knew little more than the rudiments of first-aid. They had rarely volunteered for this kind of work; they were just ordered to do it. As a result, they were not filled with an innate urge to help others as doctors are, or at least should be. They did not even belong to the army medical corps; they were just ordinary infantrymen, who were, of course, unarmed and who carried field-dressings in their ammunition pouches.

I often saw stretcher-bearers sweating and exhausted, having delivered one load, go out again through another artillery barrage to the place where they knew that more wounded soldiers were lying waiting to be picked up. Frequently there would be enemy soldiers among those they brought back. This was discipline, utter devotion to duty and complete disregard for personal safety. Their courage was not in killing men but in saving their lives. All the sophisticated methods of modern war-surgery available at the time depended upon the casualty being treated as quickly as possible. These methods could not have been employed without the unstinting efforts of these unsung heroes.

Furthermore, the morale of the fighting soldier can easily be undermined if he has the feeling that he will be left abandoned, should he himself become a casualty. A soldier under fire will think of himself and his task first and will be less concerned with wounded comrades around him. Perhaps all he can do is to put a bandage hastily over the wound of his pal. It can be truly horrifying for him to see seriously wounded men with their brains, intestines or bones protruding from gaping wounds and to hear the cries of his stricken fellow soldiers.

However, medical corps personnel must take all this in their stride. Instinctively a wounded man feels a certain sense of security when he finds himself in the hands of stretcher-bearers or, better still, of a doctor. This is in spite of the fact that he knows that the medicos cannot protect him or themselves from the exploding shells. As for the medicos themselves, like their patients they have an innate fear of death yet it is their duty to inspire the wounded with a calmness which they themselves have to fake only too often.

The medical officer in the trenches or at his first-aid post would often have to improvise splints on fractured limbs and place makeshift field-dressings over wounds. This sounds comparatively simple. However, to find a wound on a mud-covered, dirty soldier at night with no light is not exactly easy. The equally dirty hands of the doctor had to search for the spot where most of the blood apparently came from and to put the bandage there. It was impossible to wash the blood from one's hands and I frequently felt utterly frustrated about my inability to help.

One night I was called to a spot where a heavy mortar bomb had exploded amongst a group of soldiers. It was pitch dark, and wounded men lay all over the place. One of my orderlies tried to help me by shining the light from his small electric torch but it took no more than thirty seconds before this drew an intense artillery barrage aimed at us. So no more light was permitted in the trenches, and even when a soldier wanted to smoke he was not allowed to strike a match.

Our post was now filled with casualties. The question then arose as to how to bring them to the rear out of the reach of the enemy guns. Here again our *panje* carts proved useful. With their small Siberian horses they could go anywhere. I had already experienced first-hand how it felt to be strapped on a stretcher on such a cart. At the Somme, though, we were confronted with unrelenting artillery fire. The men could fling themselves to the ground or into shell-holes when they heard incoming fire, but what about the horses? These poor beasts had to stand still, completely unprotected. Their nostrils quivered, their bodies trembled and sweated and they pricked up their ears as though they could sense the approaching danger. I even had the feeling that they came closer to us as though they were begging for our protection; and all the while, their brown eyes instinctively showed a fear of death.

Many of the horses were mares who had just foaled. These tiny creatures with their long legs trotted alongside their mothers who were pulling the carts. Once I saw the stomach-turning sight of a wounded mare with her intestines hanging out, galloping over the battlefield itself with her foal running alongside her.

The animal horror continued. A mare had been harnessed to one of the *panje* carts and sent out to bring back wounded soldiers. Her little foal, just a few days old, was standing beside her. A shell splinter killed the mother, and we saw how the foal tried to suckle from the dead mare's udder. What should we do with the foal? In the middle of battle it would be impossible to bring it back to the trenches and to feed it artificially. There was nothing else to do but put a bullet through its head. So mother and child lay dead together, victims of a cruel war. There ought to be an international law to prohibit the use of innocent animals in bloody conflicts between human beings.

In spite of the unremitting artillery fire, more *panje* carts came to the forward positions. Our stretcher-bearers went out again to haul back the wounded, amongst whom were many British soldiers from a Highland division, all wearing their kilts.

A wounded medical officer was brought in, his hand smashed to pulp. He had been trying to extricate a casualty from underneath an iron girder when another shell hit the bunker and he himself had become trapped.

The motto of the German Army Medical Corps was *Aliis inserviendo consumimur*. This would translate as, 'Devotion in the service of others'. More than 1500 German medical officers were killed during the Great War putting this principle into practice. Indeed, members of the British Army Medical Corps were proportionately the most numerous recipients of the Victoria Cross and over 1000 British MOs lost their lives. The only two Britons to be awarded the double VC until the end of the Great War were both from the Medical Corps. Its motto is *In arduis fidelis* ('Faithful in adversity').

What remained of our regiment was relieved after ten days on the front line. Battalions were led by second lieutenants and companies by sergeants, and we marched back to the railhead of a narrow-gauge railway. From there we were taken in open trucks to a so-called rest camp, but this was a misnomer as there would be no rest there for the men. They had to clean their uniforms and weapons and to wait for reinforcements, before being sent back into the 'mincer'. I was posted to a heavy artillery battalion. It was with rather mixed feelings that I had to return to the hell from which I had just escaped.

It was not easy to contact a German fighting unit in the middle of a pitched battle, or *Grosskampf* as the German reporters called it. The battalion and its batteries were constantly on the move to the most dangerous places in the line, where the enemy was threatening to break through. As the formation did not belong to any particular division or army corps but was under the direct command of GHQ, nobody really knew where it could be found.

Telephone calls had to be put through to the top artillery commander. I became rather unpopular with overworked signallers, who had to try repeatedly to connect me with forward GHQ and then with the artillery commander of a division to which my new battalion had been provisionally attached. The division kept changing its position and so did the command of the battalion of heavy howitzers.

Finally, when I did get through to the adjutant, the line went dead. Signalmen were sent out from their shelter to find and repair the wires □ all this to help a very junior MO find his unit. Once the line had been mended the whole procedure had to start all over again, but I finally located my unit and marched off with my belongings on my shoulders. In the midst of a raging battle the motto has to be *Omnia mea mecum porto* ('I carry all my belongings with me').

An obliging officer from an ammunition convoy gave me a lift on a *panje* cart to the outskirts of a large village which was under heavy artillery bombardment. I waited long hours until after midnight another *panje* cart from my new battalion picked me up and brought me to the HQ in the cellar of a house which had been razed to the ground.

In daytime, burning villages emitted thick clouds of smoke. At night, the battle zone resembled a gigantic fireworks display of Very lights, gun-flashes and deafening whiz-bang sounds. Added to this were the flames of brightly burning houses and haystacks. All this made for an awe-inspiring and infernal vision, in which men had to fight and die. As medical officers, we had to tend their wounds, look after them or give them the feeling they were not forgotten because a doctor, helpless though he might be, was at hand.

The enemy kept the road junctions under constant fire. During any short and unpredictable interludes infantry regiments would rush along; horse-drawn guns and heavily-laden ammunition convoys had to gallop over roads made almost impassable by enemy fire. Parties of stretcher-bearers were stationed by especially dangerous crossroads, because we knew there would always be plenty of work for them there.

All the while, enemy aircraft buzzed overhead on reconnaissance missions, bombing raids or as fighters. Often they would attack our balloons. The latter would float motionless in the sky, with an artillery officer in the gondola, connected by telephone to the battery commanders. The balloons were tethered to the ground by long steel cables, which ran over securely anchored wheels and from there to motor-winches mounted on lorries. The lorry's engine was kept running ready to be engaged in a hurry as long as the balloon was in the air. This was because enemy fighters would often dart out of cloud to try to shoot down the balloon with incendiary rounds. These proved highly effective in blowing up the hydrogen-filled balloons. I saw for myself how, in a matter of seconds, one enemy fighter destroyed four balloons in a row before itself being hit by machine-gun fire and being forced down.

I reported for duty at my new battalion. The adjutant took me to the major at the forward command post. However, he proved far too busy to talk to me and after a quick handshake ordered me to make a round of the gun emplacements to familiarize myself with the terrain and location of the batteries.

The battalion's three batteries were firing flat out. I watched the gunners bringing up the shells in wicker baskets, each weighing about three hundredweight. It took four men to lay each shell on a sort of conveyor. The shell would then be lifted to the breech of the barrel so that it could be loaded from a horizontal position. The gunners then used a long pole to ram the shell firmly into the barrel before fitting a brass cartridge behind it filled with silk bags of gunpowder. The breech was closed and the barrel tilted to about sixty degrees to allow the gun to fire over a ridge. Accuracy was achieved by means of the head gunner aiming through a kind of periscope lined up with a pole some fifty yards behind the gun.

The men took cover, plugged their ears with their fingers and the trigger was pulled from a distance. However, the recoil was so great that the barrel shot back at least five feet. Although it weighed several tons, the gun itself literally jumped a foot or so into the air. It then needed twenty to thirty men to move it back into position. One could see the shell leaving the barrel at tremendous speed. After it had travelled in a steep curve for about five hundred yards, a small black cloud came from the shell to show that the fuse was set.

In terms of whether the shell had hit its target, the officers at the observation posts advised the battery commander in this regard and aiming adjustments were made accordingly. The battery officers worked rather like navigation officers in that they used finely-detailed charts. These maps showed individual houses, land features and the few trees that remained. Additional aiming information was provided by observers in balloons and by specially trained artillery officers in slow-flying aeroplanes reporting from overhead of the target area itself. Coded wireless signals were used to relay such intelligence. Later, I was able to use a set of powerful binoculars to look far behind enemy lines and see for myself the thick black clouds of the shell explosions.

Naturally, the enemy did his best to silence our heavy guns. However, to knock out positions behind a steep ridge required a missile landing from above and falling with an almost vertical trajectory. To this effect, enemy aeroplanes were sent to drop bombs or to strafe our batteries with machine-gun fire. This in turn necessitated an effective alarm system on our side to alert us of approaching aircraft and then required the ability to shoot them down with ack-ack fire and machine guns.

I went into the caverns hewn out of the chalky soil and listened to the observers' incoming messages and the orders emanating from battalion HQ. I had no idea why villages such as Pozières or Bazantin were such favourite targets. Later it was found that not even the house-bricks in Pozières had been left intact. All that remained was pink dust. The village name-plate was found subsequently, and this was the only evidence that Pozières had ever existed.

At the battalion command post I saw the complicated firing charts for each gun. They showed the exact radius of each gun's range. The command post itself seemed to resemble the drawing-office of civil engineering works.

After several months of bitter fighting, the mighty Franco-British offensive on the River Somme had begun to peter out. The greatest distance of German-held ground gained by the Allies was less than ten miles. Even the ground itself was useless, devastated scorched earth □ like a moonscape. All this was at the cost of over 600,000 Anglo-French casualties. As for the generals who had ordered a land war and conducted this criminal mass-murder, they were decorated, promoted and later became peers of the realm – instead of being court-martialled and severely punished, together with the politicians who had egged them on.

Our heavy guns were withdrawn from their positions. They were taken apart and reduced to manageable units, namely the gun carriage, barrel and foundation on which they stood. It took six hefty horses to pull each of these pieces. A few of our most experienced artillery observers, who knew every inch of the battlefield, were left behind. On 13 November 1916 a new offensive was staged by the British. They had even assembled large numbers of cavalry to exploit a hoped-for breakthrough. Their attack was only partly successful. Our officers had ordered a devastating artillery bombardment, and the British offensive was also halted by appalling weather conditions on the 19 November.

By now I had gained some experience of the workings of heavy artillery. When I had to live, rather precariously, in the forward trenches, I had heard our big 'coal-scuttles' coming from far behind. In the trenches we always considered heavy artillery as a kind of life assurance. Even here, however, the losses were severe, though much less so than those sustained by the enemy infantry.

Our battalion was marched to a captured French artillery training camp and here men and officers could at last relax. My duty was to see that everyone got fit again. It was also to make sure that the large red-cross boxes containing splints and dressing material were replenished and made ready again for instant use.

Another part of my role was to vaccinate the officers and men against typhoid and cholera. This procedure turned into a kind of major operation, with all the tricks and counter-tricks that dodgers can invent. Strangely enough, it was mostly those battlefield heroes, the senior NCOs, who lacked that little bit of courage to face a tiny needle from a syringe! They tried on all kinds of excuses to avoid the injection. Finally, the commanding officer took my advice and issued an order that men could only draw their pay if they produced a slip of paper, signed by me, stating that they had been vaccinated. So I had to sit down and write out hundreds of these chits until I got writer's cramp. The vaccination itself only took a few seconds. After this, the soldiers had to present their slips to the paymaster, who stamped them □ though in the end we discovered that the paymaster himself was one of the fraudsters!

In full view of the whole battalion, the first person I vaccinated was the major; then came the officers, the NCOs and the gunners. This compulsory vaccination was repeated every six or nine months. In fact, it prevented epidemics, which in previous wars had killed more soldiers than enemy fire.

On one occasion, the officer of the ordnance corps attached to the battalion detected a problem. His staff of engineers and mechanics examined every nut and bolt of the huge monsters which hurled the big shells far into enemy territory. They thought the barrel of one gun was faulty. However, as the proof of the pudding is always in the eating, the howitzer was loaded with a live shell; everybody, including myself, had to take cover while the trigger was pulled from a safe distance. Sure enough, after the ensuing large bang, the barrel burst and the shell exploded a few yards away from the gun. The major had ordered me to be present because of possible casualties.

In effect, I was working at a kind of rest centre where I had the opportunity of establishing closer personal and social contact with my fellow officers. Apart from the ordnance corps officer, they were all reservists and mostly university graduates with widely diverse interests in art, science or literature. Our commanding officer was an industrialist from Strasbourg and a student of Asiatic archaeology; one of the battery commanders, also from Strasbourg, was a doctor of economics; another was a well-known writer, who often read his poems to me. These poems dealt exclusively with the blessings of peace. Yet another was a partner in a famous firm of publishers. He would occasionally ask my opinion on manuscripts which had been submitted to him for his evaluation. We would gather in our mess, sing and drink together and one could hardly wish to meet a happier group of young people, whose job it was now to devise the most ingenious ways to kill other men.

After due delousing, many of our soldiers went on leave and my medical orderlies had to provide them with 'love parcels', as condoms were famously known. An army dentist would come to examine all the men's teeth, though it was noticeable that the artillery battalion did not play the game of repeatedly broken dentures which I described earlier.

With just a few exceptions, all our men came from Alsace. I discussed with quite a number of them whether they considered themselves more German than French. All were highly indignant at the slightest suggestion that they were anything other than fully German. My own batman was a farmhand from the Colmar area; he had been wounded and was an Iron Cross holder. He was an elderly man, who treated me as if I were his son, and we became close personal friends. As well as looking after my uniforms, he took particular care of my horse and would often go out on expeditions at night to pinch oats and the occasional juicy carrot for him. However, his devotion to me did not stop him from using a pair of hair-clippers my mother had sent me to open a barber-shop saloon for the ranks – just what I wanted to avoid, as I did not like cross-breeding among lice!

Once, when I asked him cautiously where his sympathies lay – with France or Germany – his answer was distinctly uncomplimentary to the French and he stalked out of the room. All this confirmed my experience before and during the war as to the falsehood of the claims of the enemy propaganda machine, i.e. that Alsace was a French country which needed to be liberated from the German yoke. To induce naturally excitable and sometimes hysterical people to wage bloody war for the sake of revenge, prestige and exaggerated nationalism seemed to be a serious crime to my way of thinking and no act of glory or merit.

Chapter 6

On the Move

Our Commanding Officer received orders to prepare the battalion for transport to an undisclosed destination within seven days. Telegrams were sent to every man on leave to report back for duty at once. With the exception of three, they all arrived within a day or so. Of these three, one was ill with pneumonia, a second had had his jaw broken in a pub brawl and a third was in hospital with appendicitis. So actually not a single one ignored the order. My job was to give the men a medical examination, especially for venereal disease. Despite all my preaching and the 'love parcels' they had taken with them, two chaps needed medical attention for this condition.

The soldiers exchanged their experiences of leave and almost everyone was bitterly disappointed. The married ones found that they had become surplus to requirements; their wives had arranged their lives without their husbands and now they resented it when their menfolk wanted to have a say as well. The unmarried ones found that their sweethearts had consoled themselves with other chaps. Only their mothers and fathers were glad to see them again. However, a front-line soldier does not like to be fussed over by his parents in this way. Many visited their old jobs, only to find that they had been taken over by men who had not volunteered for war at the sharp end. So after a few days the soldiers had become bored. To make matters worse, in their search for entertainment, the primitive cinemas in the villages and small towns showed films which were considered third-rate, even in those days. The men longed to be back in the batteries and companies alongside their pals, with whom they had so much in common.

I have been asked sometimes whether homosexuality played any role but I can honestly say that, at least amongst the fighting men, this vice was almost completely absent. However, behind the front lines in the administrative offices and among the occupying troops, there were quite a number of sexual aberrations. After all, the army represented a cross-section of the male population and statistics show that at least four per cent of all men are practising homosexuals.

After the obligatory delousing ceremony at the German border, we trundled over the endless plains of Hungary to Romania. At a railhead not far from Bucharest the monster howitzers were unloaded from their specially constructed wagons, as the battery and ammunition columns marched on. The troops were never required to fight, because the Romanian army just melted away. Perhaps the only members of our battalion who were kept busy were the vet and myself. The vet had the horses to look after from the medical point of view and his blacksmiths were required to shoe them. As for me, I was needed to take care of the men. The similarities between veterinary and human care continued, in that whilst I took care of the men's general medical needs, my orderlies looked after their feet.

In the meantime, the columns of troops stretched on for miles. There were three batteries with four howitzers, each of them on three different carriages, together with baggage wagons and three ammunition convoys with their own separate equipment. Horseback was the only way I could cover the large distances required to discharge my duties.

On one occasion an officer galloped up and asked for a doctor. He had been directed to me and told me to follow him immediately to the command post of the advance corps. There I found the Chief of Staff with a huge boil on his bottom! The poor man could not sit down and had given orders to fetch the nearest doctor from one of the fighting units in the vicinity. This was because the field hospitals and casualty clearing-stations were still far away. In accordance with regulations, I had come well-equipped for the task in hand, in that I was carrying drugs such as morphine, aspirin, tetanus antitoxin, a hypodermic syringe, a small collection of surgical instruments and some bandages. The Lieutenant Colonel had to bend forward over a table, and without further ado I lanced his boil. He moaned rather a lot but a few minutes later declared himself to be feeling relieved and thanked me.

My fame as a surgeon was spreading. Before long I was called to extract a decaying tooth belonging to the army Group Commander, who was also in agony. Before I used the one and only pair of forceps I possessed, I offered up a short prayer to the Patron Saint of Tooth-pullers, whoever that might be, and believe it or not I was successful. Both the Field Marshal and I breathed a heavy sigh of relief.

After these excursions I always seemed to have trouble finding my battalion again, as they were constantly on the move. I used to wait at crossroads where I calculated they would have to pass. A dust cloud would herald the approach of the marching column. The vanguard would appear first. This comprised a party of about twenty men, rifles at the ready, and a machinegun mounted on a *panje* cart. After all, we were in enemy territory. This was the first time I had seen my battalion being mobilized, as up until then the different batteries and munition supplies had been already established *in situ*. Here and there, machine-gunners were posted to guard against air attacks but again there was nothing for them to do either.

Now they passed me in defile with all their paraphernalia. First came the Commanding Officer with his staff: the Adjutant, Liaison Officers, Veterinary Surgeon, signallers and cooks. A contraption on small wheels followed – this was the hen-house, which every reputable army staff possessed. Then came the 'milk bar', i.e. the cow, and we even had a pigsty mounted on another *panje* cart with several squealing porkers inside. On one infamous occasion, a gang of rustlers stole the pigs belonging to divisional high command and orders were issued to apprehend the culprits. There was mirth all round, but neither the pigs nor the guilty parties were ever discovered.

Then came the batteries with their gigantic howitzers, followed again by all the carts carrying the necessities of army life. This included field kitchens, a bakery, a mobile smithy (complete with anvil), a cobbler's cart, tailors with their sewing machines and the saddler with his equipment. Each battery had its ammunition convoy carrying heavy shells and gunpowder and each of these had its own service vehicles. All this meant that the battalion's progress stretched for miles. In between the battalions were the ubiquitous *panje* carts with their little horses and numerous foals running beside their mothers.

The columns of *panje* carts travelled together in groups of about thirty at a time. The first and last carts had drivers but all the rest were just roped together. In spite of this loose arrangement, the carts kept to

Stephan's father, Louis.

Stephan's great-grandfather, Dr Sigismund Sello, physician to the Prussian court.

Stephan aged about six, with his mother, Dora.

Street party in Freiburg to mark 25 years of the Kaiser's reign, 1913.

Kaiser Wilhelm II during military manoeuvres.

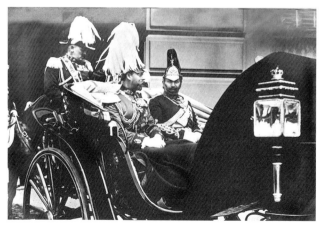

The Kaiser with his cousin, King George V.

Student days

Swimming party at Breisach, 1913.

At Breisach, May 1913.

Riverside party (Stephan standing centre).

Cadets, 1914 (Stephan fourth left). This is a
postcard sent home by Stephan from Freiburg.

Joining up, 1914.

German troops marching into Lille, 1914.

Lille under German
occupation.

German troops
and French
civilians in
Lille.

Refugees in the ruins
of Rethel.

Stephan (left)
with two
colleagues,
October
1914.

A ruined section of Rethel.

Christmas 1915
(Stephan second left).

Field postcards, for soldiers to send home

Military graves at Rethel.

A French balloon
forced down near
Rethel, October 1914.

A train amid wreckage near
St Quentin, April 1915.

Beside an ambulance train, 1915 (Stephan third left).

A triumphal postcard of St Quentin – 'here our victorious flags were waving'.

Barracks in St Quentin.

At the Somme, 1916 (Stephan left).

Stephan in 1916.

Albatross bi-plane, 1916.

Field gun in the snow, 1916.

The funeral of Stephan's friend, Captain Neddermann, Strasbourg, July 1917.

The funeral procession.

The gun carriage and coffin.

A British tank at Cambrai, 1917.

A damaged 15cm field gun.

Howitzers in action.

A moment of relaxation, May 1917. Stephan's friend Nedderman is on the left

A break for a beer.

Fasching celebrations, 1918. This scene must be taking place just as the war is coming to an end.

Stephan (standing second right) with the Red Baron, Manfred von Richthofen (seated third right), 1918.

A captured British Royal Aircraft Factory SE5.

A downed British plane.

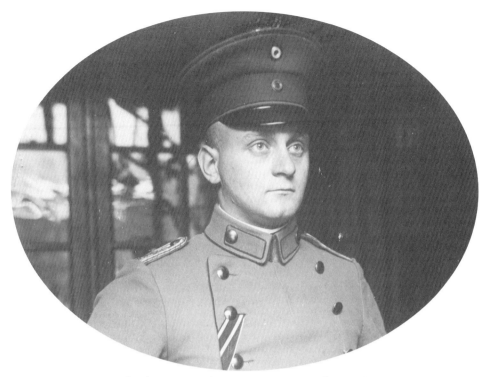

Stephan in 1918 (a postcard written to his mother).

'I was now given a horse to ride', 1918.

Stephan's ID card, October 1919. It is stamped on the back up to March 1920.

Back to medical practice, 1921 (Stephan standing third right).

Marlene Dietrich, who tipped Stephan off that the Nazis were coming for him.

Stephan in later life, in England.

a perfect military formation. The horses needed no special feeding and simply ate the grass by the roadside whenever a halt was called. An armful of hay or handful of oats would be given as a dietary supplement. Although they were never exactly groomed, the horses always looked shiny. However, on closer inspection, this was because they were covered in fleas.

Innumerable dogs attached themselves to the soldiers. One mongrel of at least eight breeds adopted me as his master. He never left my side and whether I was on horseback or on foot he would be there too. I called him Sultan. A peaceful fellow, somehow he had developed an aversion to strange horses. We were on the march somewhere when a cavalcade of officers led by some VIPs came past. Sultan appeared from nowhere and began barking like mad at the General's horse. The horse lashed out with his hooves and His Excellency very nearly kissed the ground. He was furious, and ordered the immediate execution of my faithful companion. But there is an old saying in German that you cannot hang anyone without first having captured him, and Sultan had vanished as quickly as he had appeared. The cavalcade rode on and we marched off in the opposite direction. Half an hour later Sultan re-appeared, oblivious to his death sentence, which had already been forgotten.

The people we met in the fields and scattered villages were incredibly filthy and so were their houses, or rather their hovels. Once or twice we tried to sleep in them but the bedbugs and fleas were far too hostile and legion in number. We woke in the morning covered in red spots to show just how tasty these night-time assailants had found the blood of the German soldier. When you lit a match or switched on a torch you could see the whole of the mud floor alive with armies of cockroaches, which invaded everything.

Our saddlers, tailors and cobblers had run up lengths of canvas into makeshift hammocks for us. However, they proved to offer no escape from these ingenious nocturnal torturers, who climbed up the ropes to get at us. To make matters worse, sanitation was non-existent and the peasants were completely devoid of any sense of hygiene. This reminded me of rural France, where the response to the question as to where one could answer a call of nature was, '*Tout le jardin, monsieur, tout le jardin*'.

So, like the wagon trains in the Wild West, we decided to bivouac in the open fields. We circled up the wagons, brought the horses into the middle and made our beds underneath the carts and guns. Sentries were posted at key positions around the camp, where at least we could sleep unmolested by small invertebrate creatures.

Apart from insect attacks the campaign proved bloodless and we were ordered back on to the trains and back to the Western Front. The excellent railway system and lines of communication enabled the German high command to shift whole armies rapidly from east to west or to wherever they were to be deployed. However, it had become bitterly cold and in the officers' railway compartments we were frozen stiff. The only thing to do was to follow the example of the gunners and drivers and to go on to the horse trucks where it was warm and cosy.

It was now December when we arrived in the neighbourhood of Laon. France lay under a thick layer of snow and our horses had great difficulty pulling the guns, ammunition carts and other vehicles. The *panje* horses sank into the snow right up to their bellies and all one could see of their foals was their heads popping up out of the snow.

There were no houses and we had to live in a fairly dense forest under canvas. Extra Belgian army-issue blankets were distributed, and fully dressed under four of them I would sometimes manage to keep warm. Reaching anywhere was a problem and I had to borrow an extremely tall horse which carefully picked its way through the snowdrifts. Lanes or tracks could not be dug as they would have given our positions away to the enemy reconnaissance aircraft circling overhead.

The only comfortably warm place was a largish tent which we used as an officers' mess and where we spent the short days and long evenings. Similar tents were erected for the men. Interwoven screens of brush and shrub were put up for the horses. The hardy *panje* horses stood in the open; all they needed was water and some hay. Christmas decorations were put up and the men made use of the naturally growing Christmas trees.

Then truckloads of real Munich beer arrived. The barrels were unloaded with great care, only for us to find that the beer was frozen solid. It took days to thaw them out gently and regular bulletins were issued to keep the men informed as to progress regarding this special cargo.

For heating appliances we had big stoves, into which our orderlies packed masses of coal, stolen from the locomotives parked at Laon station. For New Year's Eve we 'organized' several bottles of brandy and champagne and our cook prepared a meal fit for kings.

It was astonishing how some chefs could conjure up delicious food from next to nothing, while others could ruin the best ingredients. Happily for us, our cook was a real magician. He would provide pudding for a whole party of hungry young men with just one egg. We were in the middle of the notorious 'turnip winter', when this vegetable was the main ingredient of our diet. The bread we ate comprised dried turnip and sawdust, on to which we spread a concoction we called 'Hindenburg fat', which was itself turnip paste.

In Germany, meat was something which people could only recall from memory and even potatoes were considered a luxury. The fighting men ate horsemeat. The bread, butter and margarine situations were equally desperate. This meant that our men were fighting on empty stomachs – though many a dog disappeared – against a well-fed enemy. As far as guns, ammunition and other war essentials were concerned, the odds were also stacked against us. With this in mind, it was understandable that people smiled when a few fat pigs disappeared from divisional HQ. At least a few men would not go hungry for a short time. The soldiers could hardly be expected to understand why a general and his officers should be better off than they were.

The cooks in our mobile kitchens had adapted themselves to the conditions; they made a sort of Hungarian goulash. This comprised horsemeat and dried vegetables. The vegetables were mostly carrots, cabbage leaves, turnips, peas and even stinging nettles, the latter being highly recommended by an authority on nutrition. Working parties of soldiers were sent to gather the nettles, which were then dried and cut. Our mobile kitchens became known as 'goulash guns' and the dried vegetables as 'barbed-wire entanglements'.

One of the gunners was a veritable giant and a wrestler to trade. The German field police had picked him up for conscription in a Polish town as he was German by nationality. However, he could not speak a word of German and was constantly hungry, going round to collect every last drop of noodle soup and goulash which his fellow soldiers had left on their plates, making a *tabula rasa* of them.

Disaster struck when the makeshift chimney stack to our tent got red-hot. Our well-meaning steward had overstoked the stove and the whole surrounding canvas went up in flames. We just managed to save the brandy and champagne and joined the other ranks in their mess tents, sharing our precious drink with them.

This was New Year's Eve 1916/1917.

Part IV
(1917)

The events of 1917

10 January	Haig recommences offensive action on the Somme as a diversionary strategy for General Nivelle's planned offensive on the Aisne.
2 April	USA declares war on Germany.
9 April	British success at the Battle of Arras: Vimy Ridge taken by Canadians. Fierce resistance by Germans, and reserves brought in by evening.
11 April	British success found to be small and battle slows down.
16 April	French offensive on the Aisne begins under Nivelle. All-out attack largely unsuccessful though on 17 April Germans driven back to the Hindenburg Line (German defence line running from Arras via St Quentin to Laffaux). French fail to break through. Huge losses on both sides.
21 May	Bombardment for Battle of Messines Ridge in Flanders by Haig.
7 June	Battle of Messines Ridge, which is taken by the British. Campaign concludes 14 June.
18 June	British bombardment for Third Battle of Ypres.

31 July	Britsh infantry attack successfully at Battle of Pilckem.
16 August	Second phase of Third Battle of Ypres. Moderate British success at Battle of Langemarck. On 20 September British launch successful offensive at Menin Road.
12 October	First Battle of Passchendaele. British take the town on 6 November. Battle officially concluded on 20 November.
20 November	Successful British attack at Cambrai.
30 November	Heavy counter-attack by Germans. Losses high on both sides.
16 December	Armistice between Russia and Germany.

Chapter 7

Gas Warfare

At the start of 1917 there was a kind of semi-lull on the Western Front, broken only by the horrors of gas warfare. I received orders to report to a special training centre where medical officers for front-line troops were shown how to detect poison gas, how to ascertain the nature of the gas and how to give first aid to gas casualties.

An officer from the chemical warfare corps gave a résumé of the history of gas warfare. Poison gas had already been used by the ancient Chinese to kill or disable their enemies and in the Middle Ages a type of gas-bomb would be hurled over the walls of fortresses under siege. In 1914 the French army introduced rifle grenades containing poison gas and they were the first to use gas at Verdun, in February 1916. For their part, in 1915 the Germans blew gas from large containers over enemy lines near Ypres. However, sometimes the wind would change and the gas would come back to afflict the would-be assailants. Later, territory behind the enemy's forward lines would be bombarded with shells containing deadly gas.

In every trench, battery, camp and crossroads sentries were posted to raise the gas alarm by ringing bells or hammering on metal sheets. Everyone had to keep his gas-mask ready wherever he was: in bed or on the lavatory. The beards which some of my colleagues insisted on growing had to come off as they prevented an airtight seal with the mask. Even our horses had gas-masks, and carrier pigeons were kept in gas-proof containers.

Another officer gave us a lecture on the chemical composition of the various types of poison gas. However, I must confess that I hardly understood any of it. One can hardly be expected to make a detailed chemical analysis on the front line. The medical officers carried small strips of test paper, which changed colour according to the presence of this or that gas. Some gases were heavier than air and they settled in the bottom of the trenches or valleys and seeped into the dugouts and cellars. Others clung to the walls of the houses, only slowly evaporating and exuding deadly fumes for days.

The treatment of gas casualties was chiefly concerned with the elimination of the poison from the lungs, bloodstream and skin. The various different gases were either fired separately, or simultaneously, to 'refine' things. According to their contents the shells would fly over bearing white, blue, green or yellow crosses and containing gaseous, powder or liquid substances.

Our task was to administer oxygen to remove the oily gases from the skin. Left untreated, they would produce blisters as well as deep wounds, often right to the bone. A minute drop in the eye could easily produce blindness, quite apart from almost unbearable pain.

There was a duty rota system amongst the MOs attached to the artillery battalions and we had to take it in turns to man a first-aid post right in the middle of the batteries themselves. This forward dressing-station was in the cellar of a razed house. A few wooden beams lay on top of the ceiling but it was obvious that they offered hardly any protection against a high-explosive shell. These murderous weapons showed no respect for the small red-cross flag hanging at the entrance to the cellar.

As CO I had the privilege of sleeping on a blood-drenched stretcher instead of on dirty straw. I was past caring. There were about half a dozen orderlies and stretcher-bearers in the cellar but it was strictly forbidden by army regulations for me to mix with them. This was a pity, as I wanted to socialize with them very much; so instead of that, I became bored stiff. The only thing I could do in the semi-dark cellar was to play patience, until the cards became dog-eared and I became fed up. In the meantime, our dinner menu remained constant – it was either noodle soup or stewed horsemeat with barbed-wire entanglement.

One morning a messenger arrived and told us that an ammunition dump of mixed gas containers in a battery position had received a direct hit. The shells were still exploding and had been already causing carnage. Liquid gas was pouring out and had caused heavy casualties among the men and their officers, including the Divisional Commander and his Aide-de-Camp, who were just on a tour of inspection. We put on our steel helmets, grabbed cases full of bandages, splints, remedies for local application against the sticky gas, and syringes for injecting morphine, and ran to the scene.

Enemy artillery fire together with the mass of exploding German gas shells had turned the place into a veritable inferno. When we arrived with gas-masks over our faces we were sweating so heavily that we could hardly see through the steamed-up goggles of our masks. Their filters had become almost red-hot and they no longer protected our lungs. A dead soldier lay close by and as he did not need his gas-mask any longer I took it from his face and put it on my own. We had first to protect our own hands with bandages and special gloves, for without these we could not touch the wounded soldiers. Duly gloved, we brought the casualties to comparative safety behind a low earth wall. Among them was the General, bleeding from his arm. I applied field dressings and splints, dropped soothing liquid into the eyes of the screaming gunners and gave morphine injections without caring very much for the sterility of the soldiers' skin or of the syringe. All the time, shells were bursting around us and, to make matters worse, wooden boxes of gunpowder caught fire and produced thick smoke out of which yard-long jets of flame would shoot to envelop us.

A giant sergeant was one of my most untiring and fearless helpers. Time and again he would carry a wounded soldier to us but then his luck ran out and a shell splinter hit him in the back. He dropped flat with a casualty in his arms and we dragged both men towards us. Tearing off his tunic, I put a field dressing over his wound; that was all I could do for him at that moment. He tried to get up but could not move his legs any more – he noticed he had lost all sense of feeling in them. Diagnosis: shell splinter severing the spinal cord.

The artillery observers on the enemy side must have seen the dense smoke, and now the shelling intensified. We pressed ourselves flat to the ground, always hoping that the next shell would miss us. In the far distance we could hear the boom of the guns and after a few seconds the shell would arrive, whining, before exploding near us with a huge bang. We would then be showered by pieces of hard earth and splinters of shrapnel.

At last the bombardment eased. The men with lighter wounds limped back to our dressing-station, leaning against each other, with the fitter supporting the more severely wounded. We had to carry or drag the more serious cases over the fields full of shell-holes. In fact, these craters proved a real blessing because as soon as the French artillery observers saw any movement they sent over yet more fire and the holes afforded us some refuge.

At our dressing-station we tore off the soldiers' uniforms, which were soaked with liquid gas. As far as our very limited supplies allowed, we washed their bodies. After this they were bandaged properly and bedded down on to straw. Each man was injected with tetanus antitoxin and a large 'T' was written on his forehead in indelible pencil to warn any other doctors not to repeat the injection, as this might have had serious consequences. Like Cain in the Bible, even the General had his forehead marked.

I soon ran out of morphine. At my disposal I had two half-empty bottles of oxygen, so I could work out exactly how long they would last. Now the lung gas began to work and the men started to cough and gasp for breath. I sent one of my stretcher-bearers to the rear to fetch morphine, oxygen and dressing materials. The cellar was lit by one candle and by its light I had to relieve the seriously wounded with the one and only catheter. I quietly thanked the Franciscan monk in St Quentin who had initiated me in its use.

Ambulances and *panje* carts could not get through the incessant artillery barrages; only stretcher-bearers could make it on foot with oxygen and drugs. There were at least eighteen casualties in the small cellar in which I operated, amongst them the Divisional Commander. His Aide-de-Camp had been killed, and to make more room in our cramped hole I decided to send the walking wounded to the rear, accompanied by two of my stretcher-bearers. This created another difficulty. We had removed the gas-soiled uniforms and underwear from most of the soldiers to keep our cellar free from lethal gas. Thus they were completely naked. We gave a blanket to each of them and I lent the general my greatcoat. So His Excellency departed, complete with elegant riding boots. Some days later a note of thanks arrived, together with my coat, advising me that he himself had recommended me for the Iron Cross, First Class.

This left us with about ten badly wounded men, and my few helpers were untrained and quite inexperienced in this kind of work. The brave sergeant with the shell splinter in his spinal cord lay quiet and composed, although he realized fully what faced him even were he to survive. He told me his story, which I am sure was typical of thousands of soldiers across all the fighting forces. He was about thirty-five years old, had practised as a solicitor in a small town in northern Germany, and it was his sense of patriotism which compelled him to volunteer. He had fought in the east and the west, sustained wounds on two occasions and had been looking forward to going on leave. His wife was expecting their fourth child. He showed me a photograph of his family such as one would have found in the wallets of hundreds of thousands of German, British and French soldiers. I consoled him as best I could, but he told me frankly he did not believe a word of what I said.

It took almost two days before two motor ambulances defied the artillery barrage and arrived to remove the wounded. Our post was absolutely denuded of drugs, water, food and even candles. All our blankets had been given to our naked soldiers, so all we had to keep us warm were our greatcoats which in my case was *non est* [non-existent].

At last, after another ten days, a medical officer arrived to relieve me. When I returned to my battalion I enquired about the fate of the patients I had been looking after in our small cellar. Some of them had been dispatched to special gas-treatment hospitals but three had died, one of them the sergeant with the severed spinal cord. I undertook to write to his widow and tell her about the heroism of her late husband.

My advance first-aid station near Hill 60 in Flanders, which the Germans called the *Kemmel*, was in a small dugout, reached through a deep valley. German and British casualties filled this station, which was suddenly bombarded with gas shells by the enemy. In contrast to high explosives, the gas containers broke with a dull thud and not with a sharp bang. The fumes started to drift in our direction and the gas alarm was given. After putting on our gas-masks we found that most of the British prisoners had thrown theirs away. We had a few to spare but not nearly enough for all the British, so we packed them like sardines into our dugout and closed up the entrance with greatcoats and blankets. Several improvised tubes which we had fitted with gas filters were pushed into the space as breathing holes. To seal the entrance we wetted it with the only liquid at our disposal, namely urine. After about half an hour a breeze sprang up and drove the poisonous gas away. We removed the blankets and greatcoats with heavy hearts, fearing that our British guests would have suffocated, but they were all alive and none the worse for their incarceration.

Part of my duties consisted of visiting various smaller units which directly or indirectly belonged to my battalion. I made my rounds on horseback. Having seen my patients, I was often invited in for a drink of *ersatz* coffee, a glass of beer or wine or even a *Schnapps*. Towards evening I was mighty glad that my horse found its way back without any guidance from me. The job of men I visited was to locate the enemy batteries by measuring distance by the speed of sound. Others had to look for the gun-flashes of the enemy artillery and then pinpoint their position using trigonometry.

Some signallers were deployed to crawl on their bellies at night through the barbed-wire entanglements in front of or behind the enemy trenches. Once in position, they buried copper plates about one square foot in size. Wires connected to these plates picked up what was being said over the telephone by the enemy and sent the sound to our amplifiers. Those conducting these nightly expeditions were exposed to great danger and I had to be in the forward trenches with stretcher-bearers immediately available. All kinds of diversions were used to distract the enemy sentries' attention from the spot where the copper plates were being dug in. Sometimes even mock attacks were staged to deceive them.

The commanding officer of these special detachments initiated me into the secrets of their work. One listening-post had a man who had lived in France for many years and was completely conversant with various French dialects. He discovered that one French colonel would speak with his counterpart in another unit at a certain time every day. They would discuss troop movements and the installation of new batteries. Our man nicknamed him Chatterbox.

Apparently, French intelligence had no inkling of Colonel Chatterbox's loose talk, even though he seemed to give away secrets all the time. On the other hand, German signallers coded their messages, and the meaning of the words they used was changed on a daily basis. I received a message at a certain time advising me that 'wolves would be howling'. This was code for telling me that fresh supplies of bandages had just arrived, whereas the same message the previous day would have meant that our large trench mortars were about to open fire. Later, near Ypres, I found that the British not only insulated their telephone wires securely but took care to place them at least one and a half inches above the ground to discourage wire-tapping.

By means of these devices, however, the Germans found out that the French command was planning a mighty offensive on the Aisne along a part of the front known as the *Chemin des Dames*. Naturally, the German High Command had other sources to confirm the enemy's intentions, and made counter-attack preparations accordingly.

Whole regiments of engineers arrived in our sector. They converted every house and barn in the area into soldiers' sleeping accommodation without changing the outer appearance of the buildings. Hay and straw were cleared out from the barns and several floors connected by staircases were built in. Innumerable rolls of wire netting were arranged to make hammock-like sleeping accommodation. No man was allowed to leave his quarters in daylight and from the air the villages looked as if they were deserted.

Guns and ammunition were only brought into position at night. They were camouflaged immediately and the gunners went back to their barracks. Even the cart tracks were levelled out and covered with leaves and shrubs. We were only allowed to move around in the hours of darkness and I am sure that the French reconnaissance aircraft saw no sign of the increased activity on our side.

The German Command not only knew the date of the planned offensive but also the exact time the French infantry were to go over the top. About an hour before this time the French artillery was expected to bombard the German front-line positions, so these were vacated by the infantry and only a few sentries were left behind. During the night the German gunners made their preparations. Precisely ten minutes before the massed French soldiers were due to attack, the German guns and mortars opened up with everything they had, causing terrible carnage in the overflowing enemy trenches. Each and every French gun-emplacement had been located by German reconnaissance aircraft and by equipment which measured distance by the speed of sound. The French artillery was now kept under sustained and heavy fire, resulting in their return of fire becoming more sporadic and inaccurate.

In spite of the obvious failure of his badly concealed and equally badly executed offensive, General Nivelle, the French Commander-in-Chief, insisted on sticking to his plan. He drove his troops and reserves into the hail of German steel. German artillery observers told me how the French troops were pushed forward like lambs to the slaughter. With an awful predictability, they were blown to bits by the heavy and medium German shells. The observers really pitied them.

In the meantime, German reconnaissance aircraft took low-level photographs showing the French forward positions ploughed up by our shells and littered with human bodies. Patrols reported that they could not move without treading on dead soldiers. Only a very few were still alive and orders were given to send doctors and medical orderlies to save as many as possible. Like the British at La Bassée we went forward waving red-cross flags but we had barely covered half the distance between the German and French lines when the French artillery opened up, wounding several German stretcher-bearers. The French commanders must have gone crazy, because they then began a systematic bombardment of their own trenches containing the few French survivors.

The whole bloody affair was apparently too much for the French troops, and entire army corps mutinied and refused to continue the offensive. It has been said that between Rheims and Paris no more than two reliable French divisions remained, while the others staged a sit-down strike! The French army had lost about 100,000 men during the first twenty-four hours of the offensive and the soldiers called their general *le buveur du sang* – the blood drinker.

It took about five weeks for the artillery duels to die down, and during that time the heavy howitzers of my battalion went into action again and again. My CO was from Strasbourg in Alsace and he happened to be a very superstitious man. He had brought a large Alsatian dog with him which he regarded as a kind of mascot. As long as this dog was present he was convinced that no harm would befall him. However, the dog disappeared one day and the whole battalion was ordered to look for him. Even though we looked everywhere, and the field telephones got busy, there was no trace of him to be found. The major, a tall good-looking man, became morose and disconsolate, even though he was usually a resolute and tough individual. He spoke about his impending death, he could not sleep and I had to give him sleeping-pills. Then he began drinking, and I frequently found him drunk; something he would never have tolerated among his subordinates.

Three weeks went by and still no sign of the wretched dog. The major had to inspect a battery position and asked me to accompany him; though contrary to regulations, he went without his steel helmet. When the sound of an incoming shell was heard we raced into a ditch and I shouted to him to fling himself to the ground. The shell burst, showering me with earth. I found my CO lying on the ground with his head torn open and his brains hanging out. He was still breathing but the size and nature of his wound told me there was really no hope for him. I put a field dressing round his head and ran to the nearest post, but when I returned with a stretcher-party, the major was dead. Doubtless it was a coincidence, but his superstition or premonition had actually come true. We took his body back to battalion HQ and I placed him in a hastily made coffin. He was then taken back to his home town of Strasbourg, where he was buried with full military honours.

By the way, Sultan, my Romanian mongrel, had absconded before we were entrained for France. Perhaps he had heard of the noise on the Western Front or that many a dog had vanished there, only to reappear in the form of a fricassee.

A few days after the death of our Commanding Officer a captain was appointed to lead the battalion, a man we all knew as the commander of one of our batteries. He was a Professor of my old University in Freiburg, where he taught philosophy. He was a jolly old fellow who did not mind being the target of a practical joke. A connoisseur of good drinks, he often received shipments of famous Black Forest *Kirschwasser* (cherry brandy), which looks like water but burns like fire. One of our young lieutenants who was also a Freiburg graduate had the bright idea of swapping the contents of several bottles for clean spring water. He removed the corks from the bottles with the utmost care, drained off the *Kirschwasser* and substituted it with water. Naturally, we drank the real *Schnapps* with great delight before recorking the bottles, which now contained water, and replacing them in the captain's quarters.

We did not have long to wait for an invitation from our Captain to join him for a kind of cocktail party. With his face a picture of innocence, he served us with what looked like *Kirschwasser* from one bottle after another and we too were obliged to keep our faces completely solemn whilst praising the excellence of the *Schnapps*. The Captain himself could not suppress a twinkle in his eye when he saw all of us pretending to enjoy the stuff.

He once made a bet with one of our youngest officers that the lining of the pockets of our army-issue trousers was waterproof. The greenhorn had to put on a pair, together with his riding boots, before the Captain poured a whole bottle of cheap German sparkling wine or *Sekt* into the trouser pockets and roared with laughter when the riding boots overflowed.

Another officer of my battalion composed a marching song called *Das Gänselied* [The Goose's Song], which became as popular as 'Lily Marlene' in the Second World War. He later became the Mayor of the charming little town of Meersburg on Lake Constance, the tourist destination of countless thousands of visitors.

So you see, there were no sourpusses and our lives contained their lighter side away from the sordid battle scenes and sights of death. We were still so young and we all hoped that life would hold better things in store for us apart from killing and maiming.

The batteries and men of the battalion were taken by train to the Belgian town of Ghent, where another motorized battery of long-barrelled cannon joined us. The administration of such a mass of heavy artillery had to be streamlined and a reorganization took place which left me redundant. The batteries went into action as single units and it proved impossible for me to be with all of them at the same time. Although I was still a member of battalion staff, I was constantly on my way from one battery to another.

One of them was in action near Passchendaele in Flanders, where the battlefield was, to put it mildly, atrocious. The men sank in the mud to above their knees, the guns to their axles and the horses to their bellies. Here the British tried to break through towards Ghent and Zeebrugge, the main German U-boat base. The whole offensive got stuck in this quagmire and the losses sustained were truly awful. Sixteen years later, when I went to Edinburgh, I found a statue to the British Army's Commander-in-Chief sitting proudly on his horse, wearing long riding boots. This seemed to be the right attire for the General who lost so many men at Passchendaele and who allegedly never went near the battlefield himself. His long boots would probably have only just kept his splendidly tailored riding breeches from getting muddy.

One night I had to ride my horse over a 'road' which led across the morass and which consisted merely of railway sleepers laid next to each other by Russian prisoners of war. Our column came to a halt because a heavily laden horse-drawn wagon had slid off the passageway and blocked it. Efforts were made in the pitch darkness to harness twenty horses to pull the wagon back, but these were in vain. It was decided to push it off the road completely.

More shells were landing close to me, and my horse jumped around in fright. I had to keep it steady and calm it down though I did not feel very calm myself. Red-hot shell splinters often a foot long hissed and flew in all directions and I took cover behind a solid-looking wagon with my horse. At last the column started to move and when daybreak came I saw that the wagon was fully loaded with Very lights. One spark would have blown the lot sky-high. Apparently my lucky star was still in the ascendant.

My next journey took me to the neighbourhood of Cambrai, where the British were attacking with tanks for the first time. Our observation posts were perched on a slag-heap several hundred feet high. Steep staircases with makeshift handrails led to the observers' dugouts. When the gunners opposite aimed for these posts the whole heap turned into a thick cloud of black smoke and the men looked like coal miners coming up to the surface after a shift down the pit.

I watched the German artillery hitting the tanks and taking them out at point-blank range. This was the first attempt by the British to enclose human beings in thick steel impenetrable to machine-gun bullets. However, they would not protect them from German field-artillery shells. Nonetheless, the German infantrymen almost panicked when they saw these huge steel monsters coming towards them, flattening barbed-wire entanglements and rolling over deep trenches. They ran over men mercilessly, pressing them to the ground, leaving behind crushed and flattened remnants of what had been human beings just a few seconds earlier. All the poor footsloggers could do was to throw a bunch of hand-grenades under the tanks and hope they would blow up.

In fact, the British had broken through the German lines and British cavalry rode into Cambrai. However, they did not know how to consolidate their success, and shortly afterwards the German counter-attack followed to recover all the ground lost plus about ten thousand prisoners of war and many burned out, wrecked tanks.

I talked with some of the British tank crews wounded in action. They spoke of their high hopes as they went into battle, which they assumed would bring decisive victory.

Chapter 8

The Soldier's View

From the ordinary soldier's point of view, the general situation for Germany looked quite promising. The Russian armies had disintegrated after the dismal failure of the Kerensky offensive. Kerensky was followed by Lenin, whose first and foremost aim was to make peace with Germany and Austria. So huge German forces became available for the Western Front and Austrian heavy artillery appeared in Flanders and northern France for everybody to see.

The front-line soldiers were kept fully informed about the facts by means of official bulletins and army papers, which appeared in Lille, Brussels and St Quentin. In addition, the daily national and local newspapers arrived regularly and could be bought in kiosks a few miles behind the firing lines or with the post to the most forward positions. There, in the gun emplacements, one could find conservative papers, liberal publications such as the *Vossische Zeitung* (broadly equivalent to the *Guardian*) or the *Vorwärts* (the counterpart of the socialist *Daily Herald*).

Thus it was pointless for the British Royal Flying Corps to drop thousands of leaflets on an almost nightly basis over German lines. Printed on very thin paper, they told the German soldiers about the disastrous defeats inflicted on the German armies by the victorious Russians or the major advances made by the British breaking through the German lines. As the soldiers could see for themselves, these accounts did not quite tally with the facts as presented by the German papers.

However, what the German soldiers could not and did not realize then was the state of the reserves and the ever-growing difficulties in filling the gaps in the German lines. On the other hand, and not to mention the French, we knew from the tales of prisoners of war that Britain was in the same position. The average British soldier was just as fed up with the bloody war as the average German soldier. The only hope for the British lay with the Americans, but it would be a long time before they would join battle.

Our newspapers gave full reports of the attempts to engineer a mutiny made by ultra-leftist elements among the sailors in the German battle fleet in Kiel. The attitude of the German fighting men was to hold these attempts in utter contempt and to condemn them completely. The sailors were seen as having done nothing for years and a mutiny would be seen as a stab in the back of the front-line soldiers who faced death from morning to night each and every day. The same applied to strikers at ammunition works in Berlin and Brunswick led by Fritz Ebert, the man who would become the German Republic's first President after the war was over. Our soldiers had the feeling that their own fellow countrymen were depriving them of vital supplies, including shells and bullets with which to keep the enemy away from the Fatherland, for which so many had given their lifeblood. Here again they drew comparisons between themselves and the few pence they earned each week and munitions workers drawing hundreds of marks per week.

Then came the offer of peace by Germany to the Allies. One had only to see the gleam of hope in the eyes of the German soldier to realize his deep desire for an end to the apparently ceaseless bloodshed and slaughter. Everybody spoke about the prospects of peace negotiations and I am sure that if a kind of truce had been arranged, not a single shot would have been fired again from any German gun or rifle.

The Allies' reply was chilling. Led by the virtually fanatical Welshman, David Lloyd George, they refused even to consider the tentative German proposals. Their conditions were such that no German government would have been able to secure ratification of such a peace treaty by the *Reichstag*.

So the gleam of hope in the soldiers' eyes and the smiles around their mouths gave way to a hitherto unknown look of hatred, indicating a hard determination to go on fighting to the bitter end. Many British and French parents lost their sons because of their leaders' decision to press on with the war even though it had run its course, so to speak. Reasonable men should have sat round the table to thrash out the differences between the peoples they were supposed to represent, and not sought to foster their own personal or party ambitions.

I had to digest these facts and ideas not only for myself or for discussion with my fellow officers but also in my official capacity as an information officer. The German High Command deemed it necessary to appoint such functionaries to keep up morale among the soldiers and at the same time to be aware of their thoughts and feelings. So for each larger unit a commissioned officer was entrusted with this task, in addition, of course, to his normal duties. If one considers that an infantry company usually had only one officer, then one can understand that the regimental doctors were considered to be just the right type of person. They had a university education and were, like general practitioners in peacetime, in close contact with the rank and file.

Padres were not available for this kind of office because each infantry division had only one chaplain and the furthest forward they went, except at the very beginning of the war, was to casualty clearing-stations or advance field-hospitals. There they did good work in visiting the wounded and burying the dead. Further to the rear, they conducted church services or the funerals of high-ranking officers. As the soldiers had no real contact with them, they were not suitable. Moreover, the soldiers adopted a certain reserved attitude towards the padres, whom they did not consider to be of their own number.

It was different with the medical officer. He had to be with them in the thick of battle, attending to their wounds and ailments and often producing a successful outcome. With this in mind, personally, I had the feeling that they accepted me as one of them. They saw on my uniform a little metal badge with an embossed helmet and crossed swords indicating that I had been wounded in battle. They also saw me wearing the highest decoration the Kaiser could bestow on a man up to the rank of a corps commander – the Iron Cross, First Class.

As a rule, any private soldier or NCO decorated with the Iron Cross, First Class would be promoted automatically to the rank of sergeant. When I saw photographs of the 'New Prophet of the German People', later to become the 'Greatest Strategist of All Time', one Adolf Schicklgruber alias Hitler, wearing an Iron Cross, First Class, I became suspicious. This was because I had read that he never rose above the rank of lance corporal in the Great War. Extensive research after 1922 to try to ascertain when, where and how he won his medals (incidentally, it was not possible to win an Iron Cross, First Class without first having won the Iron Cross, Second Class) showed that it had never been awarded to him. After the Nazis came to power in 1933 further research was forbidden. My guess is that he bought it in a pawn shop to enhance his man-of-the-people image: someone who had fought for Germany with great distinction, even though it was not his native land.

So the gunners, riflemen, troopers and sappers poured out their hearts to me and told me their worries. A wife would be taken ill and I would have to write a letter for the husband recommending compassionate leave. A girlfriend would be expecting a baby and I had to arrange for the soldier to be allowed to marry her as soon as possible. Another would show me a letter from his wife stating that she could no longer stand being faithful to him as a grass widow. Her neighbours had taken in men in the dual role of lodgers and lovers and what would her husband say if she were to act in the same way? On the other hand, the German government was worried about the declining birth-rate and the demographic consequences of husbands being away from home for such a long time. It fell to me to recommend 'love leaves'.

During a short course in Brussels we were instructed by professional psychologists and politicians of all persuasions on all such topical problems. Others taught us how to lead discussion groups. We received printed guidance on a regular basis dealing with day-to-day issues and also large-scale pictures and maps showing the events of the recent past and the positions of the various battle lines. We had to prepare display cases near the front or in the camps to show these pictures and maps.

The discussions I had with the soldiers were quite interesting and revealing. The rank-and-file soldier was free to read newspapers and there was no attempt to indoctrinate him. Only information classified secret was withheld from the national newspapers, which were not otherwise censored.

I sensed a certain undercurrent of leftist opinion for the first time. Voices began to be raised. Some said the blame for the continuation of the war should be laid at the door of the incompetent generals and those controlling high finance, interested in prolonging the war for their own sakes. The point was made that the owners of the big armament companies were clinging together, afraid that an armistice or peace agreement would bring bankruptcy and disaster to their businesses.

Now we come to the United States' entry into the war. American lives had been lost during the German U-boat campaign but – and in this all parties were agreed – American bankers had made huge loans to the Western powers and thus had strong financial interests in an Allied victory. Moreover, we heard of repeated offers of large monetary investments having been made by the US to Germany. The *Reichsbank*, however, had declined them; Germany had no intention of waging a war of aggression and internal war loans could easily have been raised which would have sufficed for a short defensive war. If the *Reich* had accepted the money, reluctant as they were, the Americans would probably not have thrown in their lot with the Allies. The money men sat in Wall Street and the poor soldiers had to bleed and die in Europe.

We discussed President Wilson's Fourteen Points at length and generally we found them acceptable [these were the US President's peace proposals, which were more lenient to Germany than the Versailles Treaty which eventually emerged in 1919]. No German soldier wanted to occupy Belgian, Russian or Northern French territory. They hated the sight of it. As for Alsace-Lorraine, a modus vivendi could be found such as giving the region autonomy. A suggestion by right-wing groups to retain the iron ore mines of Briay was utterly condemned by the soldiers whose lives were at stake.

One of the keenest debaters I knew was a gunnery sergeant. He had been transferred from the navy due to redundancy, as were many sailors who had been serving in the North Sea. The naval artillerymen manned the guns which were mounted on huge railway trucks and fired deep into the enemy's hinterland. This man had taken part in the Battle of Jutland, known as the Battle of the Skagerrak to the Germans. He told us of the severe losses to the British and German fleets, which we already knew from official bulletins.

However, although the British lost almost twice as much tonnage as the Germans and about twice as many men, the fire-power of the British was still such that the Germans could not risk another encounter of this kind. Our Naval Sergeant claimed that this was the result of the failed plan to expand the German fleet. The intention, he said, had been for the German fleet to be ten to sixteen times larger than the British but the plan had only been partially executed .

Lengthy discussions ensued and the disastrous consequences of the naval blockade against Germany were debated. Germany was hemmed in on all sides: in the west by France and later by Britain and in the east by Russia. Her sea communications had been cut by the British Navy. If this could have been prevented by a kind of gentleman's agreement between the German and British fleets, the hunger and famine of the German civilian population could have been averted. However, we considered it to be part of the Allied strategy, to starve the Germans into submission and undermine their morale.

While on leave in Berlin I visited the Charité, the big teaching hospital, taking part in lectures on children's diseases. I saw for myself the havoc wreaked by hunger and starvation among babies and small children, even though such innocents could hardly have been accused of starting the war. Yet their big heads, sunken eyes, lined faces, protruding ribs and bellies and rickety legs were all a damning indictment against the much vaunted European ideals of humanity and culture.

In the obstetrics clinic, the professor explained his opinion as to why a dreaded disease among pregnant women had ceased to exist. He was speaking of eclampsia. I remembered vividly before the war seeing women writhing as if in electric shock. They would have to be held down (with great difficulty) by a whole team of doctors and nurses. The patient would grind her teeth and could hardly breathe, as one attack followed another. Her pulse became weaker and weaker until at last she entered a deep coma, with a rattle in her throat, and would not respond to any stimulus.

The professor pointed out that it was significant that since the blockade of German ports such cases had become so rare that he could not find a single one to demonstrate to his students to teach the necessary corrective treatment. Several years after the war, the incidence of eclampsia began to rise again. Why? Dozens of theories were put forward. Each idea had its own strengths and weaknesses but we do know that if the doctor detects the first warning signs of this terrible affliction, he can nip it in the bud by putting his patient on the starvation diet of German women during the Great War. So at least there was one consolation for all the political machinations of that era!

Returning to the subject of our discussion groups, posters appeared everywhere showing soldiers how to attack enemy tanks. The tanks' weak spots were highlighted and soldiers were shown how to crawl under such monsters and fix explosive charges to their undersides. The German high command gave these instructions out generously but ordinary soldiers asked what on earth prevented them from having their own tanks built. Hindenburg and Ludendorff completely underestimated the importance of these decisive weapons. Whereas it only took the British 141 days to develop the tank, the German army barely possessed a single one. This was even though they had captured British tanks galore and these could have been copied with ease. Mind you, if you ever have to deal with a general, you will find that most are still fighting the previous war. After all, the British tank was not the brainchild of high-ranking soldiers, it was forced upon them by a civilian, namely Winston Churchill.

I had to give a report on the trend of the discussions to the military centre in Brussels. However, I felt certain that the pigeonholes in this special department were full to overflowing and that the German High Command would take very little notice of their contents. In my view, the morale of the German soldier at the end of 1917 was pretty good. Nonetheless, it was a sorry sight to see them coming out of their forward positions dirty, covered in mud and thoroughly exhausted. They had to be in the trenches for weeks on end, constantly under artillery fire, facing death, always alert and living on food which could best be described as lousy.

What was it that drove the German front-line soldiers back to this inferno again and again? After only a few days' rest in a demolished village, they would report back for duty in the full knowledge that their chances of survival were extremely low. In answer to this question, a number of factors spring to mind. Of course, there was a sense of discipline, but even this cannot last forever. Then there was team spirit, so highly cultivated in the German army. No soldier could let the side down and what would his fellow soldiers think of him if he did? Next came pride in being part of a hitherto victorious army against which the whole world had fought in vain – not only the Russians, the British, the French but also the brown-skinned men from India, the blacks from Africa and the yellow-skinned men from Indo-China [S.E. Asia]. Last but by no means least, there was patriotism. This was often sneered at but was nevertheless of great importance to the ordinary man and officer when it came to sacrificing themselves. I put this point to the soldiers in my discussion group and they all agreed. They considered themselves as a kind of shield between the enemy and their own country and the folks back home, of whom they were so proud and whom they loved so much.

One might regard the love for one's country and its very soil to border on the mythical and predestined – an innate atavism. However, whenever the men spoke of their *Heimat*, the place they came from, their eyes sparkled, even though they often conceded that they were born in ugly industrial townships or villages. Nonetheless, 'home' was something for which they all longed and which they were willing to defend to the last.

This phenomenon goes back to our remote ancestors and the Latin word *atavus* means 'great-grandfather's grandfather'. We even find it in some of our domestic animals such as dogs, which will attack anyone trespassing on their territory. So it might have been with our remote ancestors, who had to defend their hunting-grounds for fear of being deprived of them and thus sentenced to death by starvation. Even some bird calls have been explained as warnings against potential intruders on their territories.

We asked ourselves, what could be the motives of ignorant coloured natives in attacking and killing us in the most cruel manner? They were brought thousands of miles to Europe in order to be used against us. Certainly their behaviour and even their bravery had nothing to do with patriotism. I once asked a wounded Senegalese soldier this question. He spoke good French and told me that it was mostly money which prompted them. He added that in almost every attack on German positions they were doped with rum. We often found the bodies of German soldiers who had obviously been tortured and mutilated before death, and the troops responsible came from Africa or Asia. We discussed the consequences of training savages in handling modern firearms and giving them free rein to use them against cultivated Europeans when they still had the mentality of the Stone Age. It did not take long before their masters reaped the harvest of this 'education' sown in the Great War.

The British and French propaganda services, or departments of psychological warfare as they were later known, had a poor understanding of the intelligence of German soldiers. They rained leaflets down on us trying to convince us of the hopelessness of winning the war or even of survival. They invited us to desert and attached small coupons guaranteeing decent treatment as prisoners of war. Only a few were weak enough to succumb to these temptations and those who did told us after the war that the British kept their promises as gentlemen, but the French did not. They treated deserters appallingly: they beat them up and French women spat in their faces or scratched them. When they tried to defend themselves they were punished severely and brutally.

Moreover, for a soldier to desert was not quite as easy as one might first imagine. There were three possibilities: firstly, deserting by going forward but this involved crawling through the barbed-wire entanglements. Then the would-be deserter had to cross no-man's-land with the risk of being fired on by his own side or by enemy sentries – quite a few died this way. To desert during a patrol was equally difficult. The company commander and his NCOs were quite good psychologists and they usually sensed when a man had set his mind on going over to the enemy. As a rule he separated himself from his comrades and this behaviour would rather give him away. Having aroused suspicion, he would not be sent out with a patrol. Instead, he would be watched by his fellow soldiers or platoon leader.

The second possibility was to try to engineer an escape to behind the German lines. However, vigilant military police would be waiting with their watchdogs, to scrutinize everyone and to ask anyone why he was there and for his written pass. They immediately cross-checked each word a would-be deserter might give. For deserters, there would be absolutely no kid-glove treatment, let me tell you.

The third way was to report sick. It was incredible the lengths to which some went to obtain the necessary certificate from the doctor. One of the most common complaints was 'frequency of urination' and this presented the MO with a difficult problem. Unless one put the man under strict observation it was usually impossible to prove whether he was faking or not. After all, conditions in waterlogged trenches are apt to cause all sorts of bladder and kidney trouble. I would not have dared to make a definite diagnosis and other MOs in the front line would also not be competent to deal with cases like these. So the man got his ticket to go to the next casualty clearing-station and to report to a real surgeon there, or better still to a urologist specializing in such ailments. This surgeon often realized at once when he was dealing with a false complainer. Yet in order not to give the man any reason to believe that he had been found out, he would administer a light local anaesthetic and pass a long thin metal tube along the urethra and into the bladder. By means of a tiny electric lamp he would inspect the interior of the bladder through a kind of periscope. This procedure was hardly pleasant and our dodger friend would think twice next time before having to undergo another cystoscopy.

As 1917 drew slowly to a close, the staff and artillery of my battalion moved back to the suburbs of Lille, to the same place where I had been billeted in a brothel in 1915. In the meantime, the military police had seen to it that these houses of joy were brought under official control, in strict accordance with army regulations, of course. An orderly from the medical corps now had to inspect callers before and after their visits and the MO had to conduct bi-weekly examinations of the ladies – in short, everything was done exactly as planned by someone in high command.

On the other hand, there were dozens of freelance prostitutes. These included the mistresses of rich industrialists from Roubaix or Tourcoing, serving the German officers as a business sideline. Generally, the authorities preferred to turn a blind eye to this type of black market but when two young officers from my battalions contracted VD I had to report the matter. The Security Police investigated the matter and the men and women concerned were sent for treatment. Both men survived the war and married. Many years later one of them came to me with his wife, complaining that they were not blessed with children. Whilst I knew why (his wife was unaware of the reason), it was not my job to give away professional secrets.

Another problem which fell to me to solve involved a French undertaker. This reputable gentleman had to bury the corpses of several well-to-do people, and such funerals in France were formidable affairs. The whole church had to be draped in black, the hearses decorated with flowers and drawn by at least two horses which also had to be in black. However, it was at this point that arrangements had ground to a halt. The undertaker's two horses were so weak from lack of fodder that once they had lain down they were unable to stand up. So he was using a kind of contraption consisting of two broad canvas belts slung under the horses' bellies and connected by pulleys to the ceiling of the stable. Thus he could suspend his horses and let them rest without allowing them to lie down. The only fodder they received was potato peelings and an occasional armful of straw or hay. This was hardly enough to sustain them, let alone enable them to pull a relatively heavy hearse.

So the funeral director came to me. I am not sure why, but perhaps because he saw that our two professions had much in common. After all, these gentlemen sometimes have to deal with our mistakes! I thought things over and went to the CO of our battery with its many dozens of horses.

We reached an agreement: the German artillery would lend the French undertaker two of its horses in return for payment in kind as rent, i.e. a dozen bottles of real French champagne, a quantity of good brandy and several bottles of wine for the soldiers. Furthermore, the two men who would have to walk in the funeral procession to the right and left of the horses had to be German gunners. Two sturdy German chaps were therefore required to dress in the livery of the undertaker's firm, with knee-length breeches and with three-cornered hats on their heads.

Everything went well and the bottles arrived just in time for New Year's Eve.

Part V
(1918)

The events of 1918

21 March   German offensive opens on the Somme, succeeds in pushing back the British.

28 March   Second phase of the offensive from Arras aiming to reach Boulogne repulsed by the British. German offensive closes on 4 April. Germans tired, suffered enormous losses.

9 April   German success in Flanders attacking on a twelve-mile front from Armentières to La Bassée Canal. German right flank is beaten back but the centre puts to flight its only opponents (exhausted Portuguese divisions overdue for relief). German advance checked by one Scottish division and only gains three and a half miles.

16 April   Germans capture Messines Ridge.

17 April   German attack resisted by the Belgians.

24 April   Renewed German Somme offensive fails.

29 April   German bombardment in Flanders; assault smashed.

May□July   German plan to draw the French south to isolate the British. Successful advance north of Aisne to a point only 56 miles from Paris met by US forces, and a halt called to the offensive 3 June. Two German offensives now in preparation – Rupprecht against Haig in Flanders and a further offensive against the French. The latter fails and at the counter-offensive in July German defence collapses, causing Flanders project to be abandoned.

August☐ November	Allies on the offensive. 8 August British offensive to free Amiens☐Paris railway successful. Further Allied successes throughout August, September and October.
29 September	Ludendorff maintains armistice essential.
1 November	German defence cracks in the north and fights a rearguard action. By 6 November French reach Ardennes.
9 November	Germany proclaimed a republic.
10 November	Kaiser leaves for Holland and is followed by the Crown Prince.
11 November	5.00 am Germans sign armistice for cessation of hostilities at 11.00 am that day.

Chapter 9

The Spring Offensive

I spent the first hours of 1918 in a French brothel. However, it is only right to point out that this was strictly in an official capacity!

Suitably lubricated by the French undertaker's wine, a group of our gunners wanted to crown their New Year celebrations with a visit to the Temple of Venus. There they met a like-minded group of Bavarian soldiers rather full of Munich beer who, according to tradition, were in the habit of rounding off a jolly evening out with a first class pub fight. In the Upper Bavarian Alps a Saturday night without a free-for-all did not really count; beer mugs were used as weapons and gashed heads, broken noses and bruised bodies were a familiar sight and a source of steady income for the local doctor.

So a battle royal ensued between our Alsatian gunners and the Bavarian highlanders. In the end, nobody knew what it had all been about. Chairs were broken and used as weapons, tables were hurled through the air and smashed against the wall-mirrors – so essential in the furnishing of such an establishment. When the *mam'selles* tried to separate the fighting-cocks they received rough treatment including black eyes and bruises. The orderly of the Medical Corps tried to intervene and he too got a thrashing.

The only reasonable thing to do was for me to join forces with the MO of the Bavarian battalion to sew and bandage up the brothel heroes and to smooth things over with the ladies. Next morning, our joiners and saddlers came to try to repair the broken furniture. It was really only junk anyway. Madame the proprietress carefully avoided telling the military police, fearing that her business would be declared out of bounds to the German troops, as this would have meant bankruptcy and loss of livelihood for her. Our CO, however, had the chaps put on a charge and a few hours' square bashing and arms drill did them a lot of good.

The question of sexual relationships between the young, and often not so young, German soldiers and French and Belgian women was a rather difficult one to reconcile with the strict rules and regulations. Our front-line soldiers came into contact only very spasmodically with the opposite sex. The country was completely denuded of its male and female civilian population for miles around and their only sight of women was the pictures of pin-up girls which they tore out of magazines sent to them by their friends or which they bought in the kiosks immediately behind the front lines. The walls of the dugouts and gun emplacements were plastered with pictures of young, seductive girls. Whilst they were never completely nude, they were revealing enough to bring the young soldiers' blood near to boiling point.

A high-ranking officer made a surprise visit to a battery position, where he found the walls covered with this kind of picture. I watched him and was rather surprised that this middle-aged man was much more interested in the pin-up girls than the serious, though admittedly, unromantic firing charts.

Even though we were also men, after all, curiously enough most of us doctors were immune to the effects of these pictures on our sexual desire. I discussed the phenomenon with several of my colleagues and they all agreed with me. Probably we knew the reality that lay behind this kind of posed picture though personally I do not like this kind of image or pornographic books and magazines. However, I honestly believe that they are a necessary evil for large sections of society of all ranks. They seem to fill a gap in the mental structure of our society and to condemn them out of hand is nonsense. In fact, appearing as an expert witness many years later I was astounded when I had to listen to a learned judge talking about them as though they were the work of the devil. I wondered whether His Lordship himself enjoyed them behind closed doors.

The Army Medical Corps Command gave these matters a lot of thought. Millions of young men were involved and it was their task to keep up both the physical and mental strength of the troops. One way out was the establishment of official brothels but these were few and far between and a long way behind the actual battle zone. We knew how sailors on the great battleships and male prisoners reacted to having sedatives mixed in their food but it was feared that this might diminish the reactions and alertness of the fighting men. I am afraid that these problems were never solved in the course of the Great War. Deeply traumatic battles causing death and injury to young men were interspersed with long periods of boredom and waiting for things which never actually happened.

When a fighting unit returned from combat and came into contact again with civilians, their dreams of houris were shattered. Instead of the voluptuous virgins of dazzling beauty as promised to pious Moslems, they found ugly, dirty, worn-out middle-aged whores, who in no way resembled the gorgeous pictures of the pin-up girls. The oldest prostitute I met was a woman over seventy with lice in her hair. When they did meet a good-looking young woman, it was amazing how the red-blooded young German soldiers could restrain themselves from committing acts of rape but their discipline was of a high order. This was in contrast to that of the Congolese French troops whom Poincaré sent into the Ruhr five years after the war to squeeze millions of marks for reparation from an already exsanguinated Germany.

There was no fraternization, strictly speaking, between German soldiers and the French or Belgian civilians. Instead, there were many examples of 'paternization' and 'maternization'. Some troops had been kept in the same place for years and when the order came for them to leave, really heart-breaking scenes took place between the departing soldiers and the women and children they had to leave behind. Later, at the end of the war, when the German armies retreated in full order, many Frenchwomen and their children left with them, sitting on top of the ammunition or provision carts. They were more afraid of what their own countrymen would do after the Germans departed, as they risked being beaten up, having their hair cut off and being put, so to speak, in the village stocks.

A set of rather complicated circumstances arose in one of the units I looked after when it came to light that a soldier had fathered babies by both a mother and her daughter. Poor frail humanity!

The enemy was of course aware that there were storm clouds building ahead of the mighty German offensive in the spring of 1918. So they tried to find out what the German plans were. We all knew that spy rings existed and were warned to guard our tongues and to report any suspicious approaches from any quarter.

I found myself billeted near Lille in the house of a high-ranking French officer, who was doubtless doing his best for his country on the other side of the barricades. The house gave out an aura of chastity and respectability and seemed almost like a nunnery. Every wall was adorned with pictures of the absent owner, his father and, presumably, his grandfather, all resplendent in their uniforms. They stared down from the walls like watchdogs waiting ready to jump out of their frames on anyone who dared to violate the sanctity of the house.

My middle-aged hostess could hardly be said to be attractive. However, her reserve gave her an air of dignity and all she ever deigned to say to me was, *'Bonsoir, monsieur le docteur'*, to which I replied, *'Bonsoir, madame.'* Late one night she asked me into her apartment because she felt ill. I found her in bed and she complained of all sorts of aches and pains – all at the same time. During the examination she suddenly embraced me passionately. I could not help comparing myself with the biblical Joseph in Egypt and Potiphar's wife and I became equally anxious to extricate myself from the situation.

As I detached myself from her clinging arms I saw the photograph of her stern-looking husband standing on her bedside table. I pointed out my position as an enemy of France, her country, and spoke to her of her husband who, God willing, would eventually return to her. This had the opposite effect to the one I intended and excited her still more, so that she bemoaned her solitary state, her yearning for sexual fulfilment and her empty days and nights. I regarded myself as somewhat compromised, remembering the end of Joseph's adventure [he was cast into prison] and I remained unmoved. This produced a complete volte-face. Now she rained abuse on me and called me all the names under the sun, including that of a heartless *'Boche'*.

In view of my status as a doctor I thought the right thing to do was to ask for a new billet but when the adjutant of my unit insisted on my giving a reason for this request I gave a tactful version of what had occurred. Laughing heartily, however, he told me that they knew all about this nymphomaniac and that I was not the first nor would I be the last of her victims. This took me down a peg or two, as I had flattered myself that it was my personal attractiveness that she could not resist.

However, on hearing that she had called me a *Boche* the adjutant became furious and even talked of informing the Military Police of what he deemed a serious affront to an officer. However, he abandoned the idea when I pointed out how these undignified revelations would look in court.

Then another thought crossed our minds: might this woman have anything to do with the spy rings of which we had been warned? The adjutant rang the security officer at HQ and told him what had happened, and sure enough, they already had her under observation. I shudder to think what would have happened to me if I had fallen for her. When I heard that my good landlady had been arrested I felt even more deflated by the idea that the real intention of this shrewd mockingbird really had nothing to do with her infatuation for me. In reality she was just a decoy, using old tricks to seduce German officers and then to compromise and finally to blackmail them into giving away military secrets.

It should be noted that the exact origin of the word *Boche* is obscure. The term was later also applied to the Germans by the British in a derogatory sense, as though the word 'Hun' was not enough.

The spring of 1918 was approaching and with it hopes were rising among the German soldiers that the bogged-down armies would soon be on the move to bring about a speedy end to the war. They saw large forces assembling. These had been freed from their commitments on the Eastern Front and brought with them Austrian troops with their celebrated and feared heavy Austrian howitzers.

One might say that as a doctor I was in a rather detached position from which to observe the preparations for the big German spring offensive. New roads were built by hundreds of thousands of mainly Russian prisoners, together with those from Britain, France, Romania, Italy and all the other nationalities which had come into contact with the Kaiser's army.

The deception practised on the enemy artillery observers worked to perfection. Half the new German large- and small-calibre batteries were kept constantly on the move, firing a few shots into enemy territory at night. When, next morning, British or French reconnaissance aircraft flew over to photograph the new battery position, there it was – or at least that was where it seemed to be – though it actually consisted of farm-cart wheels and wooden beams, all enticingly semi-camouflaged.

The British artillery would open up on these dummies, only to find that the following night a new battery would pop up unscathed a few hundred yards away from the original.

These conceits went on for weeks and especially in those parts of the front from which no real attack was planned. The enemy became restless and wanted to find out more about the troops occupying the sector opposite. So the Germans did not exchange the old troops for new ones, who might have given the game away were they to have been captured subsequently. The field batteries stood fully loaded and aimed at points where the enemy was expected to go over the top to reconnoitre in strength. Our gunners stood ready to pull the firing lanyards at any time of day or night to launch the first shells whenever they saw the right signal. These signals were multi-coloured Very lights shot from the advance observation posts. Even the colour sequences of the Very lights were changed on a daily basis to fox the enemy observers.

The heavy guns of my battalion had been tested on special artillery ranges to correct possible faults resulting in deviation from their intended true course. Every two or three hours, messages with meteorological data came through with the latest atmospheric pressure readings and the exact wind conditions, i.e. its direction and speed.

So everything was being made ready for the big attack on which the outcome of the war depended. I had been hoping to go into battle with my old comrades but a few days before, let us call it, A-day, I received orders to report to the CO of a battalion of infantry storm-troopers. They were preparing to assault the enemy's forward positions to break through and to clear a path into the enemy hinterland for our infantry divisions to follow.

My successor had already arrived. He was some years older than me and had previously practised as a children's doctor in Hamburg. Fresh into army service, all he knew of the war came from newspaper reports or crude cinema-reel footage. I had to take leave of my CO, who had become a close friend, and I also wanted to introduce him to the man who was stepping into my shoes. The new man had never sat on a horse and so we had to use a small dog-cart to which was harnessed my own charger, originally a cart-horse, by the way. The Quartermaster wanted me to use a *panje* horse at first but these were wild beasts prone to biting and kicking anyone they were not used to and always full of fleas, so I turned the offer down.

We drove along a road jammed with marching columns, supply convoys and ambulances returning with wounded soldiers. Just when we had reached the centre of a village, the Royal Flying Corps paid a surprise visit, flying low and dropping most unpleasant Easter eggs. I turned the cart into a field and we drove as fast as our good horse could pull us until we reached a type of solid-looking outhouse, behind which we took shelter and waited for the end of the bombardment.

However, the high-pitched whistle of bombs racing towards us, ear-splitting explosions, rat-a-tat-tat of the machine-guns, shouting and crying of the men, dust clouds from masonry collapsing into the streets, crash-bang-wallop of anti-aircraft guns barking furiously at the aeroplanes, pom-pom-pom of cannons firing tracer bullets and finally the plunging of a British aircraft into a field close by where it burst into flames, all gave my colleague a terrifying first impression of war. He began trembling, his face became ash-grey, he was bathed in sweat and actually started to be sick. One really ought to be broken into the horrors of front-line life more gradually, rather than being subjected to its full fury in just a few seconds.

I did my best to comfort the poor man. To try to calm him down I told him that the incident he had just witnessed was really most unusual. I hope that he believed me at the time. He would find out for himself in due course that I was a liar. Nevertheless, we had to go on to the advanced command post of the battalion which meant returning to the now burning village. There we found quite a number of casualties and were able to lend a helping hand to the surgeon stationed at the first-aid post. So my successor passed his baptism of fire.

The new battalion to which I had been attached consisted of hand-picked young men. Each was a first class athlete who had been trained fully in swift, silent movement and how to throw hand-grenades (carried in two bags in front of them) with deadly accuracy. Instead of rifles per se, they had twelve-shot automatic pistols mounted on wooden stocks. By means of a clever device, the weapon could be fixed on to the end of the holder, thus turning it into an easy-to-use rifle. Spades with keenly sharpened edges were used as side arms and these inflicted terrible wounds. The only thing a French or British soldier could do when attacked by these devils was to throw down his weapons and put up his hands as quickly as he could. He had met the 1st XI of the Kaiser's Army.

The German attack was on two sides. The first was opposite the British Fifth Army, through which the storm-troopers broke on 21 March 1918. The second attack was launched on 9 April and my new battalion was part of that spearhead. After a short but terribly intensive artillery bombardment they smashed into an unfortunate division of Portuguese troops who should have been replaced by a British army unit the previous day. The battalion raced in. My orders were to go with the first wave and to establish forward dressing-stations in the wake of the advancing troops.

As luck would have it, in a concrete machine-gun post I found an abandoned Portuguese dressing-station with a brand-new sterilizing instrument made in England. Just what the doctor ordered, so to say! I snaffled it straight away and carried it out in its brown canvas case against my stomach. After about a hundred yards a shell burst quite close to me. A large splinter of metal flew in my direction and promptly struck the metal sterilizer which I was carrying. The machine stopped the impact and whilst it received a serious dent, it undoubtedly saved my life at the price of a few bruises near my navel. I still cherish the sterilizer and use it quite often in my practice.

The war was over for the poor Portuguese soldiers. They emerged from their dugouts in droves with their hands up but as soon as the NCOs of the German engineers corps spotted them they were given shovels and ordered to start repairing the roads. Others were used as stretcher-bearers and had to carry their own wounded to my forward dressing-stations. The Germans had hardly any casualties. The Portuguese looked rather strange in their light blue uniforms and corrugated tin hats which looked like dustbin lids. From an aesthetic point of view, the French steel helmet was undoubtedly the finest. The British had what we called upside-down soup plates and the German steel helmet was modelled on that of a medieval knight.

Our good old *Pickelhaube* was a leather helmet with a brass cone on top. It was obviously designed to withstand sword slashes in cavalry attacks in the nineteenth century but was utterly useless in modern war conditions. It gave no protection against rifle bullets or shell splinters; on the contrary, pieces of stiff leather or brass ornament were frequently found in the brains of wounded soldiers and the consequences of acute brain and tissue infection and rapid death were all too often apparent. As I have said already, the generals were usually living in the past and fighting previous wars □ not the present one.

From a psychological viewpoint, a soldier wearing a steel or even a leather helmet has an instinctive feeling that his head is being protected. In his subconscious mind his main concern is to protect his brain, leaving the other parts of his body as of secondary importance.

The assault battalion stormed on, only to be fired at occasionally, and by German guns. This was because a stupid artillery observer who ought to have been with the most forward troops had lagged behind and thought the soldiers he saw through his glasses were British or Portuguese. This brought forth a monumental volume of curses and name-calling from those affected. I followed behind the leading wave of troops with my stretcher-bearers and medical orderlies. Someone had found a whole column of fully-fuelled British army lorries. Our battalion platoons swept through the countryside without finding a single enemy soldier. The way to the Channel ports lay open. The road which led through the forest of Hazebrouck to St Omer and Calais was ours.

Companies of our battalion's storm-troopers passed through the wood and a few units of the follow-up division emerged on the north-west edge of the forest. However, many of the rest simply failed to appear or turned up unfit for combat, i.e. dead drunk. They had found huge stocks of wine and spirits. Each man had taken a bottle of whisky or the like and downed it eagerly as if it were lemonade or *ersatz* coffee.

Thus the German offensive had ground to a halt on our part of the front at least, not due to lack of fighting spirit but to a superabundance of Scottish drinking spirit instead! This was certainly something Ludendorff and his staff officers had not foreseen. Now, too late, they gave orders for all the wine vats to be hacked open and their contents emptied on to the ground. Whisky and liqueur bottles had to be broken one by one, with an officer and at least three men plus a machine gun present to ensure that not another German soldier got a further taste of the stuff.

Near Merville on the River Lys we came across a British aerodrome. We found dozens of aircraft which had been piled up and deliberately set on fire, having been doused in petrol and torched. The German advance had been so rapid that there had not even been time for the aeroplanes to take off and get airborne. A little further down the road was a large and deserted British Army Medical Corps depot. The officers and their orderlies had also apparently left in a tearing hurry because we found half-eaten food on their plates. In the depot itself we discovered crate after crate of dressing materials: bandages by the thousand, real cotton and masses of gauze.

For months the German doctors had been obliged to use crêpe-paper bandages to dress wounds. The crêpe paper was about as useful as lavatory paper would have been and lasted about as long. Instead of cotton wool, we used a kind of cellulose paper, which also got soaked in no time with blood and pus and just dissolved into a wet stinking mass. In one corner of the depot I found innumerable boxes of rubber gloves; a distant memory for us German medical officers. Rubber hardly existed any more in blockade-bound Germany and the German navy even had a large unarmed mercantile submarine built to fetch rubber, copper and other essential war materials such as wolfram and the like from countries like the USA or to pick them up from neutral vessels in remote spots on the world's oceans. As a point of interest, its name was the *Deutschland* and its captain was one Herr König.

German surgeons had to tackle dirty and infected wounds without any covering for their own hands. Their only means of pre- and post-operative scrubbing-up was a kind of sand-soap, i.e. one part soap to three parts sand. What we found at the depot were thousands of pairs of splendid rubber gloves, there for the taking. I ran into the road and halted ammunition carts coming back from the forward firing-lines. I told the NCO in charge of the windfall gifts I had discovered and what I wanted, and he agreed to help in the rescue. However, when I went back to the treasure cave I found dozens of soldiers amusing themselves by blowing up the gloves and pretending they were balloons. At my old garrison town of Freiburg I had learnt some choice barrack-square language and how to bellow orders and I put this to good use by throwing the men out and saving the gloves.

During the first few days of the German spring offensive we found hardly any British forces to oppose our onslaught, other than a few companies of bicycle-mounted troops. Our storm-troopers had overrun the British artillery positions and now we found the heavy howitzers which had made our lives so miserable. Pieces of field artillery were still aimed at the German lines but now they were deserted. Some of them were turned round by our own specially trained gunners and made to fire at their previous masters. An exact replica of one of these big guns is at the artillery memorial at Hyde Park Corner in London.

By now the British had brought up their last reserves. These were former clerks, cooks and batmen, who would have been no match for the German soldiers had the latter been sober. As it was, due to the alcohol infusion, the front froze again. Slow-moving infantry divisions took over and I had to stay with them. It was quite a while since I had served with the so-called Queen of the Battlefield, namely the infantry. By rights these poor chaps should have been called the Cinderella troops, as they had to endure all the hardships and privations going, while the storm-troopers were treated like football stars. The latter lived in comfortable quarters, travelled to the 'playing fields' in buses, did their jobs and then disappeared again. It was left to the poor footsloggers to dig in, deal with counter-attacks and endure the vengeful artillery fire of the enemy. The storm-troopers themselves were so fit and well-trained and had developed such a high level of teamwork that their casualties were almost nil. They moved like snakes over the ground. They were well camouflaged and made use of every piece of cover, so that they offered virtually no target for enemy fire. When they did reach the barbed-wire entanglements of the positions opposite they had special grenades which they used to take out the defences – dangerous folk to encounter indeed.

It was left to the rank and file of the infantry to endure attacks by low-flying enemy aircraft, tanks and flame-throwers. It was horrendous to see the poor devils literally converted into burning torches, crushed flat by the broad tracks of the tanks or blown to pieces by hand grenades in their dugouts.

I had established a first-aid post near Bailleul in Flanders. The British attacked with tanks followed by infantry. The German defensive tactics had changed: instead of clinging on to every foot of trench they just evacuated the forward positions and before the enemy had time to consolidate his newly-won line a counter-attack would be launched to turn the tables. However, we were overrun in our little dugout and the British ordered us to take off our belts and wait until they could escort us to the rear. In other words, we had become prisoners of war, guarded by three Tommies and their machine gun. After about an hour, though, the Germans counter-attacked and we were free again. Into the bargain we now had three Scottish prisoners of war. Our men were very curious to know what they wore underneath their kilts.

The opposing armies became bogged down again. Fresh trenches were dug, more barbed-wire entanglements set up, so that these horrible devices were used again. In my position as MO I had to see to it that there were latrines and that lime was handy. It was a fact of life that with shells exploding all around one often exposed oneself to danger when answering the call of nature.

The regimental commander called me to his headquarters and showed me an order from the director-general of medical services posting me to a hospital situated far behind our lines. Obviously the employment agency for probationer surgeons had decided that I deserved a break from my front-line duties. The huge hospital to which I was posted was in the most delightful setting, right in the heart of Ardennes, and consisted of several large units. When I arrived there I found that my luggage, which I had sent in advance, had disappeared. As this was the case, I had to report to the CO in my dirty, shabby uniform which I had worn for so long in the trenches with the front-line troops. My trunk was found in southern Germany and returned to me about three weeks later.

The Army Medical Corps major had never seen any fighting and his uniform looked spick and span. He kindly directed me to the Officers' Mess as I had not eaten for over thirty hours. An orderly in spotless whites received me and led me to a table covered with an immaculately clean cloth. Then a Lucullan feast cooked by the chef of one of the most famous restaurants in Strasbourg was placed before me. As I tucked greedily into the food, I was unable to suppress guilty thoughts of the front-line soldiers eating horsemeat or meagre rations of Hindenburg fat made from turnips.

After dinner, I found my new colleagues. They were all elderly men and were engaged in a game of skittles in a purpose-built bowling-alley – probably constructed to imitate the thunder of wartime cannon fire!

The doctors greeted me most warmly and even lent me a razor to shave off my three-day-old beard. Then the chief instructed me as to my duties. The hospital was a small general one for inpatient cases or for minor surgery, for which a consultant surgeon had to be called from the nearest larger unit. There were many sawmills in the area and quite a number of workers presented with deep cuts on their hands. An occasional case of appendicitis was also admitted and here the consulting surgeon gave me the chance of operating under his guidance. A physician would be called in for medical cases because it so happened that all the resident doctors were specialists in psychiatry.

The large central part of the building was a mental hospital housing hundreds of patients suffering acute psychosis, shell shock and other psychiatric ailments. The block was staffed entirely by monks of a nursing order, each one a powerfully built giant at least six feet tall. The patients were kept in large wards. Unruly patients were often put into padded cells, where they stood in an agitated state, talking constantly to themselves or to people or things which existed only in their imagination. Others had hallucinations, still reliving the horrors of an artillery bombardment or gas attack. They covered their faces with their hands as if to protect themselves from shell splinters. Others would shout out for their gas-masks which they could not find and still others heard voices under their bed-covers threatening them with death.

The lack of modern drugs and methods such as shock therapy compelled the doctors to put some violent patients into straitjackets of strong canvas, fastened at the back by leather straps. These had long sleeves which crossed over the chest and were also secured at the back by leather straps. One man pleaded constantly with an imaginary foe not to run his bayonet through his stomach. Other patients would be put for hours into lukewarm baths to calm them down.

The giant monks stood in the corners of the wards on constant guard duty watching every movement of the inmates. Most had lost control of their body functions and were doubly incontinent. They wet their beds and would smear excrement over their faces. Others stared blankly into space for hours, days or even weeks, and needed force-feeding.

I would first have to call a warder whenever I walked through the long corridors and wanted to enter a ward. The warder would open the door for me with a key which he carried on a steel chain around his waist. The doors would close automatically and nobody could leave without the help of a warder in possession of the right key. Quite often

I would be called at night to one of the patients and would have to walk for almost a mile through half-lit corridors, never knowing whether there was a maniac around the next corner ready to attack me with some kind of weapon. It took a certain amount of nerve not to become a psychopath oneself.

Even to this day, in remote corners of the countries involved in hostilities, I am convinced that mental hospitals still house incurable cases of mental disorder caused by the horrors of the Great War.

The third block was surrounded by high barbed-wire fences. The only patients there were quite normal looking females who had been picked up by the military police in the act of prostitution and found to be suffering from venereal disease. This so-called *Damenschloss* [ladies' castle] came under my care. A specialist in venereal disease gave me thorough instruction on how to treat these cases. If in doubt, I had to contact him, otherwise he would call only once every two weeks. There was a small story associated with the staffing of this unit. At first, nursing sisters from a religious order were in charge. However, they were quite unable to cope with this bunch of completely unruly women from the dregs of society. The 'ladies' beat up the sisters, so the authorities had to bring in female warders from German women's prisons who knew how to control them. A well-meaning German women's association at first insisted that the girls should be treated only by female doctors but the patients beat them up as well. Thus male doctors had to take over and so I became one of the unfortunates to whom this onerous duty was entrusted.

One woman was like the gipsy girl Carmen in Bizet's opera. Wild and completely uncontrollable, she was suffering from the most dangerous and contagious form of syphilis. She quarrelled with everyone and fought constantly with her fellow inmates. Skin and hair would fly. A few years earlier, in 1910, Ehrlich had produced a biochemical anti-syphilitic drug called Salvarsan, and this was considered to be the best remedy available. However, our Carmen lady vigorously refused treatment of any kind and when I tried to explain that the treatment was for her own good she laughed and taunted me, calling me every name under the sun, culminating in the words '*sale boche*'. She worked herself into a towering rage and finally spat in my face, to the great amusement of the other girls who were looking on. I snapped at this point and hit her left cheek such a smack that it spun her around. This did the trick. She calmed down and the other girls saw not to trifle with me.

The Matron of the female warders came to me to express her gratitude for an act which had put a stop to the girls' unbearable behaviour. Not so the Chief, to whom I had to report the incident. He carpeted me to such an extent that I have not forgotten it to this day. He reminded me of the fact that we were members of the finest profession in the world and that we had to treat our patients with respect, regardless of their standing, behaviour or nationality. It was our duty to give them proper medical treatment even under extreme provocation. Finally, I was told to remember that most of the inmates of the ladies' castle had the mentality and intelligence of six-year-old children and many were psychopaths.

In view of my war record and the nervous strain caused by it, he would not start disciplinary procedure against me. It was true that since the early days of the war I was mostly on my own, in the ambulance train, with the artillery or in the trenches and my orders had been obeyed without question. Here I was a somewhat insignificant member of the team and was finding it difficult to adapt to this role. Furthermore, my main interest was in surgery and many of my ancestors had been surgeons right back to the seventeenth century. I was not best suited to this type of work.

After a few weeks I felt that I needed a fresh start elsewhere, and after a number of strings were pulled I got a posting to the Air Force. However, just before I left we received a message announcing that we were to receive a dreadful VIP visit! It would either be from Her Majesty the Empress or one of the Grand Duchesses.

So the hospital had to be scrubbed from stem to stern. This included the bedside tables and their contents, bedpans and spittoons, which HRH might be especially interested to see. The patients were rather annoyed by all this upheaval and one of them, a Berlin boy, threatened to use the word *Arsch* (arse) were he to be asked on which part of his anatomy he had been wounded. This was deemed to be unsuitable for royal ears and his threat caused much anxiety among the medical staff.

Her Royal Highness the Grand Duchess of Hesse duly arrived and the Chief and I conducted her on a ward round. The patients had to lie to attention in their beds and did not like that at all. The high-born lady went to each of them and asked a few irrelevant questions. Most probably she had to perform this duty almost every day of the week and was bored stiff. Then she approached the bed of my *enfant terrible.* He smiled and I feared the worst. Perhaps to change the theme, and in contrast with her earlier questions to other soldiers, she asked where he was born and whether he was married and had children. To my great relief she then moved on, and our young man looked rather crestfallen!

Of course, she was not allowed near the mental hospital and was not informed that we had, horror of horrors, a ladies' castle in one of the blocks.

Chapter 10

Retreat

I was posted to the German Air Force which included the Richthofen Staffel [Squadron] of the so-called 'Red Baron'. Here the atmosphere was completely different to the rather stuffy one at the mental hospital. There were men of my own age and these were men who knew that they had to act on their own initiative to succeed in mortal combat with enemy airmen.

With these knights of the air one could still detect the age-old code of chivalry. The men belonged to a force which had not existed in former wars and they were masters of their own destinies. Of course, they were given orders and directives but once airborne they were single fighting units and had to rely on their own ability, alertness and courage as combat pilots. A sort of code of honour existed between the German and British flyers which both sides respected. It was not the done thing to kick a man when he was down, metaphorically speaking. Once the victor had made sure that his adversary was beaten he left him alone. Not so the French airmen, who would machine-gun a crashed aeroplane to kill the pilot and his observer.

This gentleman's agreement had grown up between the British and German air forces. They fired because they were being fired at and they killed so as not to be killed and, of course, because they were ordered to do so. It often happened that a British airman who had been shot down over German territory would be invited to the Officers' Mess and toasted as an honoured foe. Wreaths would be dropped for an air ace killed in combat, or the personal effects of a downed German or British pilot would float down over the airfield where he had been stationed.

I mingled with the mighty, including those who wore the highest German decoration for valour, the *Pour le Mérite* [also known as the

Blue Max]. As well as Manfred von Richthofen himself, one of these was a certain Captain Hermann Goering. Quite a number of the flyers confided in me that before each mission they were overcome by a terrible fear of death, which they had great difficulty in hiding. They would often sit trembling in the cockpit of their aircraft before take-off but once in the air this nervous tension disappeared and most of them would take on an icy calm. All the same, I had to recommend that some of them be grounded due to their state of extreme nervous exhaustion.

I had many arguments with the Chaplain. He would insist on blessing the fighter aircraft, bristling with machine guns, before they went up for the kill. I never did understand where religion fits in at, say, the launching of an atomic submarine designed to destroy hundreds of thousands of human beings. Surely this is not in keeping with the Sixth Commandment, 'Thou shalt not kill'? The Chaplain answered that the German airmen were fighting for their Fatherland, for freedom and for a better world.

Yet from my perspective, the problem was that the British, French and all the other nations involved in this bloody war were all doubtless fighting for the same ideals. Hatred did not exist between combatants: it was something manufactured by the politicians and bellicose propagandists far behind the lines of battle. Even some of the most recently published accounts of the Great War repeat the distorted fictions that the 1914□18 propaganda machines were able to pass off as fact.

When weather conditions prevented any flying we played cards for ridiculously high stakes, which nobody had the slightest intention of paying! Then followed philosophical discussions, mainly on courage and death. We all agreed that only people devoid of imagination were the so-called fearless ones, because they were incapable of picturing what might lie in store for them.

In flying conditions, we would hear machine-gun fire from high above us in the sky and, looking up, would see two or more 'planes dog-fighting. They twisted and jinked around each other, climbed and dived, and by turns were both pursuer or pursued. Suddenly one would catch fire. Emitting smoke, it would break up in the air and flutter down like a dead leaf, as one or two tiny spots plunged down towards the earth – the crew. In those days there were no parachutes or ejector seats. When they hit the ground, the bodies would bury themselves into the earth, sometimes several feet deep into the soft mashed-up earth. The medical journals published long articles by 'experts' claiming that the rapid fall through the air caused the aorta to rupture, resulting in instant death. However, at several post-mortems which I had to attend it was found that this was not the case. The new sport of free-fall parachuting proves the point. No, these poor chaps lived until they hit the ground. With the traditional grim humour of such situations, the joke that did the rounds was that specially made coffins were provided for them – very broad and very flat.

One of the units I had to look after was for long-range reconnaissance. They often flew over London in broad daylight and I saw photographs of the Thames, Tower Bridge and Buckingham Palace taken from a height of more than 19,000 feet. The aircraft were open to the elements and seemed to comprise wooden struts held together by piano wire. The sides of the fuselages of these 'orange boxes' were lengths of canvas painted grey and bearing the Iron Cross. In front sat the pilot with the single engine forward of him, whilst the observer sat behind him on a small folding stool to which he was loosely tied by a safety belt, though he was otherwise unsecured. A pistol for Very lights was the only firearm carried.

When one of the pilots invited me to go up with him in his little kite I did not take him seriously, especially as he told me he had very nearly crashed the day before. When he pressed me on the matter I relented, not realizing that he meant that we should fly that very minute and so I could not avoid it without serious loss of face.

Goggles, crash-helmet, fur-lined jacket and gloves were ready for me. Disconcertingly, before I climbed aboard an orderly wrote down the names and addresses of my next of kin – just in case! To add to my feelings of foreboding, another airman told me that a lone enemy fighter could easily swoop out of cloud to dispatch a slow-flying reconnaissance machine.

In some trepidation, then, I was strapped in. The pilot fired up the engine and the aeroplane slowly rose into the air. Once airborne, the pilot pulled all kinds of stunts: twists, stall-turns, chandelles, dives and steep climbs so that I became completely disorientated. When at last we landed on terra firma I thanked my lucky stars for the safe return. However, with this initiation behind me, I flew again but without the aerobatics. As I enjoyed it, I went on to take part in quite a number of training flights.

About a quarter of a mile from the township where the Air Group HQ was situated there was a prisoner-of-war camp. I had to attend its inmates and here I found a mixed bag of nationalities with British, French, Italian, Romanian, Indian, Portuguese and Russian prisoners. In this Tower of Babel it needed a linguistic genius to understand the patients and to make them understand what they had to do. *Bolit* (it hurts) and *kashel* (cough) were the only Russian words I had mastered, so I resorted to the international language, namely speaking with my hands.

Terrible undernourishment was the cause of many of their ailments. The emaciated bodies, with hunger-oedema and deeply sunken eyes, were an awful sight. The prisoners suffered from all kinds of sores and I did all I could for them with the very limited means at my disposal. It was pitiful to see the Russian prisoners, with their swollen and bleeding feet wrapped in rags, searching the rubbish bins for something to eat. After all, what could the hungry German soldiers have left on their own plates? The British and French, on the other hand, looked well-nourished. They received regular food parcels from the Red Cross and some even offered food to their German guards.

I suggested to the camp commandant that we should pool the food parcels and share their contents out equally between all the prisoners. This he did. The Russians beamed and some of the British and French grumbled – for them, apparently, when it came to food, the Entente Cordiale was in short supply.

As the only French doctor in the little local town had died, I inherited his civilian patients. I always carried a small pocket book, which proved most helpful in finding the right diagnosis and treatment. I now had to deal with heart and skin troubles as well as gynaecological ones. Even my vade mecum failed me quite often and I went to consult the French pharmacist on the pretext that the proprietary names of his drugs were unfamiliar to me.

In comparison to me, the midwife proved a veritable font of knowledge. One night I was called by her to a woman in childbirth and *madame la sage-femme* decided that I would have to use forceps. Finding a pair of obstetric forceps among the instruments of a flying corps doctor was a little too much to ask, so we searched the house of the deceased doctor, where we finally discovered some rather antiquated forceps. Before joining the army I had had some training at university in how to use these instruments. We had to try them out on the heads of dead babies which were inserted from above into an exact replica of a female pelvis lined with leather. We called these models 'leather virgins'.

So in the middle of the night I tried my luck and delivered a young Frenchman. Under the circumstances, I could not reveal that I was only a medical student in the uniform of a medical officer, as this would have undermined the confidence of all those concerned. Of course, I never accepted any fees for my rather inadequate services. However, the French civilians were so well supplied with rice, cocoa and coffee by the Red Cross organization that they brought me a whole hundredweight of rice. I immediately sent this in small parcels to my starving family in Berlin. Furthermore, we bartered food. What could a Frenchwoman do with cocoa but no sugar? So two pounds of artificial honey were exchanged for half a pound of cocoa and this also went to Berlin, where it was swapped again, perhaps for some butter.

I heard that my mother and some of her friends went on extended tours to the countryside, where benevolent farmers sold them meat or eggs at tremendously inflated prices. When they arrived back in Berlin, policemen stood ready to relieve them of their heavy loads, and on top of the loss of their precious hauls they were fined for infringing emergency regulations. After the war the Regius Professor of Hygiene admitted that the urban population of Germany would have perished without the black market.

Early one afternoon, I received an urgent call to a pilot officer. The man was running a high temperature and was on the verge of delirium, so that I was almost afraid to examine him. The only thing for me to do was to have him taken at once to a military hospital, where I knew that a medical specialist would be available. I accompanied him and attended the examination but the physician was as much at sea as I was with regard to diagnosing his condition. He referred to his books again, as I had done, but this proved fruitless. He asked me to wait. Three hours later the empty hospital was overrun with similar cases, as Spanish influenza had invaded Europe and many other parts of the world. This was to prove a vital influence on the war.

Whole army corps would actually be halved in number. Our own squadrons could not send up any reconnaissance 'planes because between fifty and sixty per cent of the pilots, observers and ground crew were laid up. We were unaware of the fact that the same plague had attacked the enemy lines, necessitating a halt in America's recruiting for the US army and forcing their training camps to close down. It was mostly lung complications which made the mortality rates so high and most of the victims it claimed had previously been among the strongest and healthiest.

Doctors and nurses were not immune. I developed a high temperature, severe headache and had difficulty breathing. Six aspirin and half a bottle of brandy helped me to recover – unscientific and unorthodox, certainly, but it worked. After all, this pestilence had never before been mentioned in medical publications; it had descended upon an ignorant medical profession which did not possess the means of detecting the germs or bacilli which caused it. We did not have electron microscopes nor did we know anything about sulpha drugs or antibiotics.

The Spanish 'flu ranged far and wide. It affected the whole world and accounted for the deaths of more people than Mars, God of War. Field hospitals for all the front lines were concentrated in France and I was posted to one of them. The hospital unit had come from Romania, where all except two of the doctors and all but six of the orderlies had died of spotted fever. Medical officers had become so scarce that they were moved about as stopgaps to wherever they were needed most. The German universities were producing hardly any young doctors because schoolboys were drafted into the armed forces as soon as they reached eighteen.

My new hospital was established in goods sheds near to a small railway station. When I was on duty one night, the stationmaster summoned me urgently to an accident which called for both surgery and psychiatry. A group of mostly elderly soldiers had been standing on the platform waiting for a train to Germany, either on leave or because they had been posted to factories or other formations. When the train arrived, a very athletic-looking sergeant got out and, with absolutely no warning, produced a knife and stabbed one of the old soldiers in the neck, just where the carotid artery runs. Blood gushed out and the man collapsed. As he was about to run completely amok, the sergeant was overpowered, knocked out and tied up by the other soldiers.

When I arrived, the only thing I could do was to bind the nasty-looking wound with a field dressing and to press my finger down hard on it. I continued to apply pressure to the wound as the man was carried away on a stretcher to the operating theatre. The surgeon operated immediately and found that, by sheer luck, the dagger blade had only split but not severed the almost finger-thick artery. So he was able to sew it up with very thin threads inserted so close to each other that they almost touched. The sergeant was taken to a mental hospital. I later heard that he eventually landed up in the same place in the Ardennes where I had been on duty a few weeks earlier.

On another occasion, a soldier reported that he had swallowed a bone which had stuck in his gullet, causing great difficulty in breathing. The MO on duty tried to get hold of the bone and extract it with a special instrument known as a 'coin-catcher'. This was a metal contraption fixed to the top of a long whalebone. When introduced into the oesophagus this was supposed to catch hold of the foreign body by means of a swivelling movement and to draw it out. The doctor duly introduced this crude apparatus but when he tried to pull it back out the instrument itself would not budge. The patient complained of sharp pains, began to toss about and bleeding set in. He was X-rayed and we could see the metal top sticking up from just behind his heart.

None of us knew what to do and the surgeon resorted to his textbooks on invasive surgery. He could not decide from which end to approach – from below through the stomach or from above via the thoracic cavity. However, he lacked the necessary experience and appropriate instruments for the latter method. Anaesthetic masks and Sauerbruch's hyper-pressure chambers had yet to be invented, and techniques which enabled the lungs to remain extended even after the pleural cavity had been opened and operations performed on the intrathoracic organs were unknown at that time.

In the meantime, the poor patient was lying there with the long handle of an instrument sticking out of his mouth whilst he was bleeding and turning blue in the face. After long and rather agitated discussions all round, someone had a brainwave. Amongst our instruments we had another flexible whalebone which had a small sponge attached to its end. We soaked the sponge in water and carefully introduced it so that it came to rest on top of the coin-catcher. It covered it so as to clear the way upward and so it was withdrawn, painstakingly slowly, together with the metal contraption. The bone which the soldier said he had swallowed had never existed. He had suffered a nervous spasm of the gullet and the windpipe.

In the meantime, the fighting between the British and the Germans had virtually come to a standstill, so we admitted hardly any front-line casualties. The Germans bolstered their defensive positions and the British only attacked sporadically. However, some French and British politicians who had never been near the front line themselves made dramatic demands of their war-weary troops to go on fighting to throw the Germans back. Some British units were forced to heed these instructions, went over the top and suffered completely unnecessary losses as a result.

For many years I have read *The Times* personal columns of births, marriages and deaths. I am too old now to be interested in births or even marriages; I leave this to my grandchildren, who have almost grown up themselves. I do, however, read the deaths columns with close attention, because now and then I find the familiar name of an old pal who has joined the great army above. The names of officers and men who sacrificed their lives on the many battle fronts where the British fought can be found in another column, headed 'In Memoriam'. The place names such as Festubert, Loos, Beaumont, Cambrai or Ypres include those where I fought or served as a surgeon.

A few weeks ago I found the name of a lieutenant colonel from the Irish Guards. He was a winner of the Victoria Cross, Military Cross and bar, an Officier et Chevalier de l'Ordre de Léopold, Croix de Guerre, Belge, Légion d'honneur and he was killed in action on 4 November 1918 – one week before the Armistice. I am sure that this gallant officer would have loved to live and to serve his country, had he not lost his life as a result of the orders of politicians. The same could be said of the many thousands not mentioned by *The Times*.

I spoke with the British prisoners of war who had just been brought to us. Officers and men alike openly declared that they were utterly fed up with the war, exactly as we German soldiers were. Mind you, the German front-line troops still stood firm in spite of the reports in the newspapers which still arrived regularly. These reports said that the south-eastern front had collapsed, that the Bulgarians had deserted as allies and that the Austrians had been called home by their newly formed government. The Italians claimed to have won a glorious victory at Vittorio Veneto against the Austrian forces, which were practically non-existent; those few who remained simply stuck their rifles into the ground, bayonet first, and flatly refused to fight.

The front-line soldiers saw the so-called reserves arrive – boys who could hardly hold a rifle, men who had been taken out from the rear echelons behind the lines but were too soft to endure the rigours of the open battlefield. Soldiers with unhealed wounds were sent back to the front. Still they resisted an enemy who had fresh reserves and an abundance of food and ammunition. New trenches were dug and occupied, machine-gun nests manned and obstacle after obstacle erected.

Then the Royal Flying Corps dropped millions more leaflets proclaiming that neither the British nor the French wanted to kill the soldiers who were doing the fighting. Their objective was the leaders who had brought about the disaster and who had lied for their own gain. The leaflets implored the soldiers to throw down their weapons, to surrender and to join a nobler, freer society where all men were brothers.

The German newspapers, on the other hand, printed headlines in large letters of the words of Sir Eric Geddes, First Lord of the Admiralty, that the British would 'squeeze Germany [like a lemon] until the pips squeak'. Many British and German lives were lost on account of this stupid 'lemon-squeezer'.

From behind the lines came exhortations to the front-line soldiers to heed the siren voices with their alluring promise that all men were brothers and that they would be received with open arms. We had heard all this before. 'Revenge,' cried the voices, 'revenge on the war profiteers!' They had planned this war at their sumptuous banqueting tables and stolen the bread from the mouths of the soldiers and their families, leaving them to rot away in squalor and dirt so as to be undisturbed at their own lavish festivals.

These voices shouted at the soldiers to tear the epaulettes from the shoulders of their officers who had mistreated them for far too long, to kill them and to return to a new Germany. A state of peace, welfare and love would be created. Their banner should be a flag, red with the blood of their fallen comrades.

On all street corners one could find the prophets of this faith, with red cockades in their caps and red flags in their hands. Many of them were former ammunition workers who had gone on strike and been put into uniform and drafted into the army. The front-line fighters were not very enthusiastic about this kind of talk and beat up the agitators. However, more and more red-guardists arrived and tried to set up 'soviets' of soldiers. A supply column passed through our little township with red flags on their carts. A few seconds later, a platoon of infantrymen seized the drivers, gave them a good hiding and tore down the flags.

In our field hospital on 6 November we found ourselves virtually between the two front lines. Our chief had orders to pack up and march back into Belgium, but we still had quite a number of patients with broken limbs or pneumonia for whom he had ordered ambulances to take them behind the lines. We waited and waited but no ambulances arrived. Here again the *panje* carts came in handy. We packed three or four patients at a time on top of these 'maids of all work', or we improvised stretchers which we fastened to our horses. All our animals were used to pull the heavy wagons or to carry the patients, so we had to walk and to push the heavily laden carts when it became necessary.

At a railhead we found an ambulance train under steam, ready to depart for Germany. We packed our patients on to this godsend and marched on. After four days we arrived at the small Belgian town of Hal. A civilian told us of the outbreak of a revolution in Germany and also that the Kaiser had abdicated and fled to Holland. We did not believe a word of this at first but a day later an army bulletin announced that an armistice had been concluded. According to this, the German army had to hand over all its heavy artillery and to evacuate the left bank of the Rhine.

Cries went up from London and Paris to 'hang the Kaiser'. It was Horatio Bottomley, a rather dubious John Bull character, who convinced the British Prime Minister, David Lloyd George to adopt this slogan. There would have been a nasty shock had he and the French Premier, George Clemenceau ('the tiger') tried to carry out these threats. Many German divisions consisting of experienced NCOs and the best of the fighting men would have fought to the last man rather than deliver the Kaiser to the enemy and so many more French and British would have died for this crazy idea. However, even Generals Ludendorff and

Hindenburg misjudged the high morale of the front-line troops when they persuaded the reluctant Kaiser to leave for Holland. 'Little Willie', the Crown Prince, volunteered to stand in for his father at any trial but in the end the Dutch flatly refused to hand Wilhelm over to the Allies. So the whole scheme came to nought.

Nonetheless, this all helped Lloyd George to achieve his goal of winning the 'khaki election' of December 1918. Soon afterwards, most people in Britain realized that his election platform had been bloodthirsty and absurd, whipping up emotions caused by post-war hysteria. The new socialist regime in Germany did nothing to stop this anti-Wilhelm campaign. On the contrary, it suited them nicely to discredit the monarchy.

The German armies now began an orderly retreat under the command of Hindenburg. They marched for twelve hours and rested for twelve hours. As the roads were used night and day they were not congested. Our way led us via Liège over hilly country and when the tired and emaciated horses were unable to pull the wagons uphill we all had to push. Sometimes lorries would drag two or three carts at a time on long steel ropes running over large cogwheels installed on the hill tops.

As for me, I marched in French army boots which my batman had picked up somewhere. He sold them to me as they were not his size and they fitted perfectly, indeed much better than my worn-out German riding boots with holes in the soles.

By now the hitherto uninterrupted deliveries of mail and newspapers had become rather erratic, leading to all kinds of rumours. We heard that the men of the German fleet had refused to sail their ships from Kiel, that they had mutinied and hoisted the red flag. Soldiers' councils were formed everywhere under the direct orders of the new leftist government. Even our small formation organized a soviet and the drivers and stretcher-bearers came to me, the Benjamin of the medical officers, asking me to be their chairman. I had other plans, namely to reach Berlin as soon as possible and to sit my final medical examinations. So regretfully I declined this honour, and the next youngest doctor was appointed.

The functions of these councils were very vague. Officially they had to approve the orders given by the commanding officer of a formation, but in practice they confined themselves to supervising the distribution of rations and to stamping documents. Nothing in Germany was recognized as valid without at least one stamp and several illegible signatures – whether it concerned the posting of a soldier or an application for grease for wagon wheels.

Whilst we marched east, masses of British, French and other Allied prisoners of war marched west. As we passed, a general handshaking took place between us and once again I would emphasize there was no hatred. That was only created artificially by armchair-warriors and mischief-making politicians. We crossed the Belgo-German frontier near Aachen and the local population were almost frantic in their greetings. The front-line soldiers did not have much sympathy for the new regime under Ebert and Scheidemann, not knowing that the proclamation of a German Social Democratic Republic had only just staved off an attempt by the communist Spartacists (a movement which took its name from the leader of the slave uprising in ancient Rome) to seize power and impose their brand of socialism on Germany.

The infantrymen and the artillery gunners tore down the red flags and beat up their bearers. In an industrial town, a well-known hotbed of deep red socialism, they demolished a large triumphal arch bearing the inscription 'Welcome to the German Socialist Republic'. Sirens called the workers out from the factories and a tense situation developed when the workers attempted to attack the commanding officer of a field artillery formation which was just passing through the town. Without having received any orders from their officers, the soldiers made their weapons ready to fire on the masses. It needed only one spark to ignite a massacre.

The mayor rushed to the scene and he and a number of officers managed to calm the crowds. The workers returned to their factories and the soldiers marched on, but I do not know whether the triumphal arch was re-erected.

Some of our men lived in these parts of western Germany and they disappeared without permission from our commanding officer or even that of the soldiers' council.

On and on we marched, never less than twelve hours per day. Now a new duty was assigned to me, namely that of liaison officer with the medical units and army HQ. My job was to keep them in contact with higher command and to see to it that orders reached the field hospitals, companies of stretcher-bearers and casualty clearing-stations. This was not easy with the inefficient telephone communication system and with units which were almost constantly on the move. So a motor ambulance was allocated to me but it broke down almost in sight of the Rhine. Therefore I had to cross the river on foot over a pontoon bridge with my belongings on my shoulder, just as I had done in August 1914 in the first days of the war. I waited for my formation, which arrived towards nightfall.

I was now given a horse to ride and was always in the vanguard so as to prepare night quarters for the tired troops. Often I had to arrange for entire houses to be cleared out and straw to be laid in the rooms, in order to squeeze twenty-five to thirty exhausted men into them.

Under the command of divisional HQ, assembly areas had been created, and our destination was an agricultural community in one of the most fertile parts of Westphalia near Münster. There was no lack of food here. The local farmers had grown rich on the black market and they killed pigs for us, their wives baked bread and cakes and we lived like lords on the fat of the land. We certainly ate more in one week than we had done during the whole of the last few months. We were waiting for orders as to where to demobilize, and I knew that the latest date for adding my name to the list of final examination students was 10 December 1918. In the meantime, more men absconded, some even taking their horses with them. We suspected that they sold them to the local farmers for their fares home.

As we had no advice from divisional HQ about plans for our demobilization, the chief went to Münster to make enquiries because he was anxious to return to his own medical practice in Magdeburg. He could only report that perhaps in several weeks' time we would be transported to Silesia and only then be allowed to return to civvy street. This would have shattered my own plans and so I persuaded him to let me go to Münster to see what I could do. My batman and I rode there on horseback and I told the chief of staff that our precious and dangerous drugs were being stolen and that there was a danger that they might find their way into the hands of drug-peddlers. Apparently this made a deep impression on him. Finally the divisional commander agreed to let us hand over our stuff to the Medical Corps depot in Münster and immediately demobilize the officers and other ranks of the field hospital.

With this order in my pocket, I rode back to our Chief and got him to write out my certificate of demobilization, without which I could not have travelled and worse still would not have been able to apply for a food-ration book. The whole document was merely a piece of paper torn out of an army notebook but signed and properly stamped in good Prussian style. Now I had to go to the chairman of the *Soldatenrat*, the soldiers' council, for him to add his signature and stamp. It was a little strange to see two official stamps on the same piece of paper, one with the crowned eagle inscribed 'Royal Prussian Field Hospital No 380' and the other 'Soldiers' Council of Field Hospital No 380 of the Socialist Republic of Germany'. In the left-hand corner was a large grease spot!

I sent a telegram to my mother announcing my return to Berlin. At 6.00 am my batman drove me to the nearest railway station at Neu-Beckum and here I squeezed into a train full to overflowing with soldiers. The only seat I could find was only temporarily unoccupied – in the lavatory.

I talked to many officers and men on the endless journey and almost all of them longed to start the new life of which they had dreamt in the trenches. One spoke of his old father who had kept the farm going, others talked about their wives, whom they had not seen for years, and of the changes that might await them when they arrived home. There were also students like myself, eager to complete their studies and to start their careers. For others the life of an ordinary civilian no longer appealed and they became the nucleus of the *Freikorps*, which was recruited by the Baltic barons to drive the red hordes from their estates. They would be kept by their masters like medieval mercenaries, until finally they became the forerunners of the Nazis and their brown-shirted rabble.

The train reached Berlin late at night and I dragged out my heavy trunk. Here I was on the station platform which bore the name of my home town. This was the moment for which I had yearned for so many years. First I had to show my certificate of demobilization to a sergeant with a red armlet and a red rosette on his cap. He affixed yet another stamp on this piece of paper. Then I came to the barrier and had to give up my ticket.

A notice hung there saying that officers were not allowed to carry arms and I had a dagger-like knife on my belt which belonged to a medical officer's uniform for personal protection. I found it useful on one occasion when I was attacked by a Senegalese soldier to whom I was trying to give an anti-tetanus injection. The knife had served me well for four years. I had also used it to cut the trousers away from soldiers wounded in the legs or to open tins of bully beef when I had no tin-opener. Under the notice on the railway platform stood a sentry. A mere schoolboy, he wore a red armlet and had a cigarette in his mouth, a rifle dangling upside down from his shoulder and an obsolete *Pickelhaube* on his head. He looked at me and my dagger and I looked at him and his rifle, waiting to see what his next move would be. In the end, he grew red in the face and did not utter a sound □ better for him and for me.

Then there was my mother. She had already been waiting for hours and was almost frozen stiff. She had brought with her a little four-wheeled cart on which I put my trunk. Both of us pulled it through the dark side-streets. This was to avoid the main roads because, my mother explained, of the fire-fights between the Socialists and the Spartacists.

So I returned to my parents' home almost five years after I had left it to put on the *Königs Rock*, the uniform of the Kaiser's army. My old civilian clothes had disappeared and it was impossible to buy new ones, so I had to wear the uniform for quite some time longer.

If I had hoped that my return home to Berlin was journey's end, I soon found out that I was mistaken. The following morning was the last for registration for the final medical examinations. As I walked towards the Ministry of Education on Unter den Linden I came under fire from rebel sailors who had come to Berlin from Kiel. They had barricaded themselves in the Imperial Mews and Armoury and were besieged by troops loyal to the Kaiser, who were bombarding them with artillery and trench-mortars. Just as when I was an infantryman, it was a case of taking cover immediately. When I did reach the university with my papers, the place was in utter chaos. What was left of the windows was filled with sandbags, and bullets were ricocheting off the walls. I had to go to the *Studentenrat*, the students' council, to get permission to sit the examinations. I found them in solemn conclave deep in the basement, in the ante-room of the ladies' lavatory.

There were hardly any reliable newspapers and certainly no radio. Rumours were rife that the Spartacists had killed fifty or more policemen. We felt that the shaky Socialist government was on the brink of complete breakdown. It had in no way fulfilled our hopes and wishes. The 'Dictatorship of the Proletariat' would soon be established, bringing more chaos and bloodshed in its wake. From reliable eyewitness accounts of German soldiers who had returned from Russian prisoner-of-war camps we knew about the dreadful conditions there.

Posters appealed to former front-line soldiers to come forward and form a kind of security police force to prevent further murders and civil disorder. I volunteered to join the 8th Hussars. My orders were to keep my steel helmet and uniform at the ready and to report to local headquarters when called. I kept a cavalry carbine in my cupboard at home, together with a belt of fifty rounds of ammunition and several hand grenades. These looked rather different from the harmless firecrackers which we had let off on New Year's Eve of 1913/14. I am convinced that such units prevented communism from taking over Germany. Without them, the red flag with its hammer and sickle would now be flying on the shores of the Atlantic and Pacific Oceans.

On this New Year's Eve there was no family party. Members of my family were scattered across Europe, dead. The same applied to the families of our friends. Many of the younger ones had been killed, some were in hospital and others were still prisoners of war in France, Britain or Russia.

It was forbidden to bring Christmas trees into Berlin. People had very few candles to light, no fuel to keep warm and the power stations were idle as the workers preferred to march with the Spartacists.

Almost five years had vanished since I had put on the Kaiser's uniform in Freiburg. Nearly all my pals lay buried in foreign soil, together with nine million soldiers who had lost their lives in the Great War – and for what?

Epilogue

After the First World War, Stephan Westmann qualified as a doctor in his home town of Berlin and married one of Germany's first female GPs. My grandmother was called Marianna Goldschmidt. The couple had three surviving children, all born in the 1920s: Liselotte (Elizabeth), Anna-Maria (Anne) and Ernst (my father 'Tom'). Stephan and Marianna's stormy marriage ended in divorce and my grandfather then married his medical secretary, Anne.

As Professor of Gynaecology and Obstetrics at Berlin University, my grandfather was a star young surgeon at the top of his profession with an 'A' list of clients. He owned an expensive car, a large house on Berlin's fashionable Kufürstendamm, employed servants and sent his children to the best local private school. With the Nazis' rise to power in January 1933, however, his life fell under threat

His dismay at the poisonous anti-semitic rhetoric of the Nazis soon turned to anger and he made a number of public outbursts against Hitler. The German word *heil* has the dual meaning of 'heal' as well as 'hail'. When a female Nazi Party member gave the notorious *Heil Hitler* salute, Stephan replied that he regretted that his medical training did not allow him to heal such a lunatic basket case as Adolf represented. He was duly denounced. Pro-Nazi former friends shunned him and he noticed his telephone was being tapped.

Stephan Westmann had also brought down the wrath of pro-Nazi factions in his department and elsewhere. Whilst his lectures on family planning, safe sex and women's emancipation had become popular 'sell-outs', his views completely contradicted those of the Nazis on eugenics and their wish for the propagation of the so-called Aryan race of 'pure' Germans. As if his anti-Nazi opinions were not enough to hang him, and whilst he seems never to have gone near a synagogue, Stephan Westmann was readily identifiable as Jewish and he had many Jewish friends. In short, he had become a marked man.

In April 1933, just three months after Hitler came to power, he received a tip-off from one of his celebrity patients. Marlene Dietrich was well-connected and a staunch anti-Nazi to boot. She told him that the Gestapo were about to pay him a visit and that he must flee for his life. He took the hint. On the pretext of making an out-of-town call to a medical emergency, Westmann sent his children to a safe house outside Berlin, jumped into his car with his wife Anne and headed for the border.

However, his recently serviced car broke down near Helmstedt. The repair took hours and proved expensive, though he later wrote that he never paid such a large bill with such alacrity! The final hurdle was an excruciating, half-hour-long document inspection at the road border into France at the Saar. When their passports had been finally stamped, the barrier was lifted and Westmann started the two-hundred-metre drive across no-man's land to safety. Glancing in his rear-view mirror, he saw the German official run out of his hut gesticulating for them to return. He floored the accelerator and shot across to France, where it became apparent that the German official had simply forgotten to give them back their police passes – no matter, they were free.

On arrival in Britain, they headed for Edinburgh and my grandfather sent for his five-year-old son, Ernst. In the meantime, Westmann's two other children stayed with their mother in Berlin. With Goldschmidt as her maiden name, she could hardly hide her Jewish background, and both girls were sent to a Jewish school where they were forced to wear the yellow star of David on their uniforms. In 1935 they, too, escaped and the girls went to boarding school in Sussex.

The reason my grandfather went to Edinburgh was that under an ancient by-law, the Scottish medical authorities allowed doctors with foreign qualifications to re-sit their exams during or after one year's study in Britain. At that time in England, the only accepted foreign medical degrees were those obtained in Italy or Japan. Westmann quickly brushed up on his schoolboy English and took and passed the exams which allowed him to practise medicine again in his adopted land.

As the war-clouds gathered once again in the late 1930s, he moved his practice to London's Harley Street and had a house built in fashionable Hampstead. There, his group of friends included Albert Einstein, Walter Gropius (founder of the Bauhaus architectural movement) and Artur Schnabel (the classical Austrian pianist famous for his interpretations of Beethoven and Schubert). My late father could remember peering over the banisters as a little boy at the family home in Hampstead to see Schnabel at the piano accompanying the others in lusty renditions of dubious German student-drinking songs!

With the Wehrmacht forces poised to invade in 1940, Stephan Westmann changed his name to Stephen Westman and had his family baptised. He volunteered to run an emergency hospital for British forces near Glasgow and took the honorary rank of colonel. His son Tom was sent to Epsom College with its strong traditional of educating boys for the medical profession, though flying rather than medicine was to become his passion.

All three of Stephen Westman's children served in the RAF in the Second World War. My aunts were stationed at Hell-fire Corner (Dover), where they used their mother-tongue German to 'talk-down' Luftwaffe pilots into landing on English soil. Elizabeth was also in the SOE (Special Operations Executive) and was twice parachuted back into Germany. She took the secrets of what she did there to her grave. Tom himself was selected for fighter-pilot training and gained his military wings just as the war ended.

As Stephen Westman's grandson, I was born in Hampstead in 1956 and also educated at Epsom College. Therefore, my heritage is that of someone with a foot in both camps who takes the view that his grandfather served with distinction under two flags – even though the first is still reviled in some quarters to this day as having visited mayhem on peace-loving Britain! The kindly old man I remember as a small boy was also a man of steel who gave of his considerable best in the service of two proud nations.

A century after the Great War, his is a remarkable story which is being retold in my native language of English. Stephan Westmann will appear on the BBC Antiques Roadshow website and the Imperial War Museum website. A recording of his voice was broadcast on the BBC Today programme on New Year's Day 2014 to mark the centenary of the start of the Great War. A film of his life is planned.

Stephen Westman died at his home in Chorleywood on 7 October 1964.

Glossary

Aliis inserviendo consumimur	The motto of the German Army Medical Corps: 'Devotion in the service of others'.
Atavus	One's great-great-great grandfather/ grandmother or ancestor.
Berliner Weiße	Known by Napoleon's troops as the 'Champagne of the North', *Berliner Weiße* is a sour, wheat-based, effervescent, low-alcohol beer (3% alcohol by volume) brewed and drunk in Berlin. It is traditionally served in a goblet-style schooner glass. To counteract the sourness, it is often served '*mit Schuß*', with a shot of flavoured syrup.
Bolit	Russian for 'it hurts'.
Caligula	Nickname meaning 'little boots' given to Gaius Julius Caesar Germanicus, third Roman emperor, who ruled AD 37–41.
Cuirassier	Soldier on horseback armed with a pistol.
Dulce et decorum est pro patria mori	The line from the Latin poet Horace's Odes made famous by the British Great War poet Wilfred Owen. It may be translated as, 'It is sweet and honourable to die for one's country'.
Einkreissung	The literal meaning of this word is 'encirclement'. This was a military strategy to surround an army or force and to cut it off from its supplies.

Entente Cordiale	An alliance or understanding between countries, especially the alliance of Britain and France before 1914.
Franc-tireur	A sniper in the French army.
Fräulein	German courtesy title and form of address for an unmarried woman.
Furor teutonicus	A Latin phrase to describe the 'fury' with which the Teuton (German) tribes fought in battle. The Roman poet Lucan alludes to their 'mad, merciless, berserk rage in battle'.
Gemütlichkeit	A warm and cosy feeling of well-being.
Generalissimo	Italian word for general which includes the superlative suffix to mean utmost or of the highest grade. Describes someone who commands a whole nation's combined forces or the forces of several countries, though sometimes used with a hint of sarcasm.
Gott mit uns	'God with us'. The phrase was embossed on the belt buckles and helmets of First World War soldiers. Its Latin equivalent was first used as a battle cry in the late Roman period.
La guerre de revanche	'War of revenge'.
Gute Leute bitte schönen	'Good people live here, please treat them kindly'.
Heimat	The English words 'home' or 'homeland' are a close approximation to this German word, which has no exact English equivalent.
Homer's Iliad	Greek epic poem attributed to Homer, about the ten-year siege of Troy.

In arduis fidelis	The motto of the British Army Medical Corps: 'Faithful in adversity'.
Jäger	A huntsman.
Kashel	Russian for 'a cough'.
Kufürstendamm	Taking its name from Brandenberg's Prince-Electors, this is one of Berlin's best known avenues. With many houses, the street is also home to fashion designers and car showrooms.
Landturm	Literally meaning 'land tower', to imply defence of the realm, these were regiments of soldiers deemed to be too old for front-line duty.
Landwehr	'Defence of the land'. These were units of differing numbers of recently trained men or old reservists.
Liberty Bonds	Bond sold by the US government to support the Allies to finance the First World War. Subscribing to the bonds became seen as an act of patriotic duty for ordinary Americans.
Locum tenens	A professional standing in temporarily for an absent colleague.
Love parcels	Condoms issued by the German military.
Madame la sage-femme	The midwife.
Marseillaise	French national anthem adopted shortly after the Revolution and named after the workers of Marseille.

Meurthe et Moselle	French band music used to inspire patriotic feelings.
Mineurs	Miners.
Modus vivendi	An agreement allowing conflicting parties to live together peaceably, pending a final settlement.
Moujik	Russian for 'a hard-working peasant'.
Non est	Non-existent, absent.
Pickelhaube	The spiked helmet of the German army. Worn from the mid-nineteenth century, it was something of a relic by the time of the Great War.
Poilu	Meaning 'hairy', this was a term used for French troops since the time of Napoleon, often with affection.
Prosit Neujahr	Traditional German New Year's greeting, usually involving alcohol.
Quis desiderat pacem, praeparet bellum	This Latin adage, 'He who desires peace, prepares for war', is from Vegetius, the Late Roman writer on military affairs, although the original idea can be found in Plato's Nomoi (Laws), written in the fourth century BC.
Schellenbaum	An emblem similar to that of the Roman legions.
Seidel	A large (one-litre capacity) pottery beer mug.

Tabula rasa	Meaning 'a blank slate' in Latin, the sense here is that the table would be completely cleared of all food and drink.
Tout le jardin, monsieur, tout le jardin	The answer to the question 'Where is the lavatory?' in rural France, meaning, 'You may use the whole garden, sir.'
Unter den Linden	'Underneath the lime trees' (which lined both sides of the avenue), this is the name for an iconic boulevard in Berlin. By the nineteenth century it had become the grandest and best known street in Germany's capital.
Vade mecum	Something useful which one carries about.
La victoire et la gloire de l'armée française	Inscription on posters left behind by the French army, meaning, 'The victory and glory of the French army'.
Wolfram	Or tungsten, from the Swedish for 'heavy stone'. This is a hard, rare metal used in military applications such as the manufacture of armour-piercing projectiles.
Zeitgeist	The defining spirit or mood of a particular period of history as shown by the ideas and beliefs of the time.